Competitive Intelligence

Published by Economica Ltd.
9 Wimpole Street
London W1M 8LB

© Economica Ltd, 1999

First published 1999

Printed in France

Robert Salmon & Yolaine de Linares

Competitive Intelligence
Scanning the Global Environment

ISBN 1-902282-04-3

Competitive Intelligence

Scanning the Global Environment

Preface by Jean-Baptiste de FOUCAULD
Foreword by Edward CORNISH

Robert SALMON
Vice-President of L'Oréal

Yolaine de LINARES

✳✳ ECONOMICA
London • Paris • Genève

To Lindsay Owen-Jones

TABLE OF CONTENTS

FOREWORD

Thinking about the future is essential for success in business and life in general, and today it's more important than ever because so much is changing so fast. As Robert Salmon makes clear in this wide-ranging, perceptive book, the world is undergoing an extraordinary techno-economic revolution, causing sweeping change in family life, education, and all other aspects of our society, and we must know more about these changes so we can plan appropriate strategies for achieving our goals.

To succeed in the future, we need to know more about how the world is likely to change. The new technologies now being developed promise many new changes in people's lifestyles, even as we try to adjust to the changes already forced on us by television, computers, fax machines, and microwave ovens.

By reading a book like this, we take an important step in preparing ourselves for new opportunities as well new dangers ahead. As we think ahead and plan, we discover a new power: We find that our ability to create a more desirable future increases as we think further out in time, because time is needed to accomplish great things. Rome was not built in a day, and we cannot instantaneously make big changes in our career or life situation, but we can make them by planning ahead and working toward our goals.

By thinking ahead, and working toward carefully-chosen goals, we can perform miracles, because our power over the longer-term future is truly astounding. Japan, a backward, dirt-poor nation in the nineteenth century became a world power in a few decades by deliberately reshaping its future. After President Kennedy decided to put a man on the *moon, it took only eight years to do it. Bill Gates, a university student with little but a dream in 1975, has become the world's richest man.*

Most of us are slaves of the present, chained up by the demands of the current crisis (real or imagined), but we can learn to be masters of the future, and people like Robert Salmon are showing the way.

Edward CORNISH
President, World Future Society

PREFACE

The present book by Robert Salmon and Yolaine de Linares takes the notion of economic intelligence and broadens it into the concept of competitive intelligence. Today's firms, they contend, do not only have to make efficient use of all available, relevant economic data. They must also be aware of everything going on around them, and that calls for "scanning the global environment." In a complex world in which intangible factors and human relations assume increasing importance, business success can no longer be won by applying ready-made formulas. Competitive intelligence requires agility, creativity, and proactivity.

The authors are in a particularly good position to make this point. Robert Salmon, former Vice-President of L'Oréal, has spent years traveling around the world, taking a keen interest in Asian culture, specifically Indian. Yolaine de Linares has worked side by side with him in L'Oréal's Future Scanning Unit ever since it was set up over ten years ago. Their research activity, their familiarity with what other people from around the globe are thinking about the future, and their concrete experience of working in a large, French multinational have given them an unusually broad, sophisticated vision of globalization. Rejecting the idea that globalization means uniformity, they emphasize the need to reconcile national identity and culture with the demands of an open world economy. Companies are thus compelled to understand the specific rules by which the business game is played in the various countries where they operate.

The main thrust of this book, however, is to detail the methods large corporations have to use in order to succeed in an increasingly competitive environment. Scanning involves much more than just accumulating data, especially since we are confronted today with an over-whelming flood of information. Companies must learn how to analyze and sort the information they gather, paying close attention to intangible factors that may turn out to be of great significance. This implies breaking loose from the tyranny of the short term, which often leads us to neglect what is most essential.

This analysis gives rise to a new conception of the leader, described as the "linchpin of competitive intelligence." According to the authors, leaders are not only strategists and men (or women) of action; they must also be visionaries. They have to be capable of both getting involved and stepping back. They need to have talent and to know how to stimulate the talent of others. They must combine managerial ability with charisma. In any event, the influence of corporate leaders will certainly increase in the years to come. They will be judged on the basis of the many facets to their personality, i.e. their ability to deal with complexity, to reconcile economic and social concerns, and to contribute to making our society a better place to live.

Yet the authors also convey the impression that however intelligent and competitive companies may be, they cannot solve the problems of post-industrial society all alone, any more than the market can. The question as to the goals and values of the world of tomorrow concerns everyone. It is, however, to the credit of the authors that they openly raise this question and call upon the business world to play its part in searching for answers.

It is time, they tell us, for economics to get back to basics and to become once again the science of human needs, defined as broadly as possible. Excessive materialism can only lead us down a blind alley. If we want economic growth to be a force for human development, instead of an end in itself–or even an "addictive drug" for our society– we have to give equal weight to three basic human needs: material needs, spiritual needs, and the need for satisfying human relations. In this regard, companies must find new ways to organize the time of their members, so that work ceases to dominate their identity and becomes one of many factors contributing to their personal development.

The democratic countries have been deprived of the easy target once provided by their former communist adversaries. As long as the Eastern bloc embodied a negative example, the West could avoid the soul-searching required to find positive meaning. Moreover, competition from the socialist world forced the West to improve the lot of the underprivileged in society. Today, however, the democratic nations will have to respond on their own to these, as well as to other challenges. The present book by Robert Salmon and Yolaine de Linares provides us with valuable insights as to how that might be done.

J. B. de FOUCAULD
Former French Planning Commissioner

Acknowledgements

First and foremost, I must express my gratitude to L'Oréal and its CEO, Mr. Lindsay Owen-Jones, as well as to all my colleagues there, especially Gérard Chouraqui, Castres Saint-Martin, Grollier, Lafforgue, Leprince-Ringuet, Muller, Rabain, Vachey, Valeriola, and Weil. I have learned a great deal from them, and it was with their help that Mrs. de Linares and I could develop our analyses and work out our scenarios. L'Oréal has in fact been an inseparable part of my life. Without the countless discussions, exchanges, and concerns we have shared among peers, this book would never have been written. I greatly appreciate the stimulation I received from them, as well as the unfailing support given to us by Jack Mas, Guy Peyrelongue, and Hervé Guérin.

I am also indebted to a number of forums, scholarly societies, and conferences that have left their mark on the present period. Their bold vision of the future has always appealed to me.

They include the following.

• The World Economic Forum, whose President, Professor Klaus Schwab, and Mr. Claude Smadja untiringly carry on a laudable crusade for greater world harmony and understanding.

• GBN, its President, my friend Peter Schwartz, Napier Collyns, Steward Brand, and their fabulous network, whose insatiable curiosity about promising new developments has been an important inspiration to us.

• The World Institute of Science and its leading members, especially Professors Ilya Prigogine, Jean-Marie Lehn, François Gros, and Louis Albou, who have offered us their thoughts, their advice, and their friendship.

- The Entreprise et Prospective think-tank, led by Christian Stoffaes.
- The Club de l'Expansion and the World Future Society.

A number of important figures who have influenced contemporary thinking also made significant contributions to the development of our ideas, often during conversations they were kind enough to have with us. This book owes a lot to the following people.

Nicholas Negroponte	Jacques Lesourne
Charles Handy	Gottlieb Guntern
Alvin Toffler	Gottlieb Guntern
Masao Yukawa	Pierre Nicolas
Professor Shosaburo Kimura	Jagdish Parikh

Lastly, I would like to give special thanks to my long-standing friend, Professor Antoine Faivre. For thirty-five years, we have exchanged ideas in discussions that were sometimes a bit wild, but always a major source of enrichment.

Robert SALMON

We would like to thank our colleagues at L'Oréal with whom we had the chance to hold discussions, because they have all contributed something to our thinking. We only regret that we cannot mention them all here.

We would also like to express our gratitude to the small team that helped us so generously in gathering material and editing our manuscript, including Corinna Doose, Odile Pfannenschmidt, Victoria Bonnamour, and Patrice Kobis, as well as our cartoonist Denis Meillassoux.

INTRODUCTION

We certainly won't stun anyone by stating that the world is currently in the throes of radical, increasingly rapid change. Everyone senses today that things are moving fast, that no safe predictions can be made. We are living in a period of instability, one that foreshadows the advent of a new society. Yet in this context of mounting uncertainty, where we know that just about anything can happen, we have to make decisions that will largely determine the future of our companies.

For centuries, rationalistic Western civilization has consistently attempted to slice reality up into neat chunks. This has resulted in considerable progress in scientific fields like medicine. Today, however, such a reductionist approach appears to be powerless to account for the emergence of new, complex elements that are hard to control and that constantly challenge us.

Our understanding of economic phenomena has also advanced by leaps and bounds. The trouble is that the traditional forecasting and planning methods were suited to a situation of steady growth occurring within a stable institutional framework. After the era of certainty, which culminated in the three decades following World War II, we suddenly find ourselves caught up in a period of great turbulence in which information is fragmented and events are exceedingly difficult to interpret.

Radical change raises
the level of complexity.

Whatever business your company is in, the quickening pace of change has disrupted the competitive game. What follows is a list of a few of the radical changes that have taken place in the past several years.

• Globalization.

• The meteoric development of information and communication technology.

• Deregulation and fragmentation of markets.

• The blurring of the boundaries between industries and the arrival of "new entrants" on traditional markets.

• Significant shifts in consumers' needs, expectations, and dreams, which are both the cause and the effect of the new context of change and uncertainty.

The combination of these factors obviously has tremendous impact on the standards of corporate success and the definition of competitive strength.

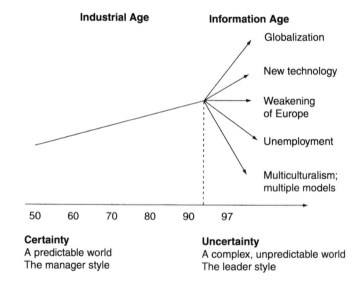

Sudden shifts and chaotic situations become more and more likely, while the increasing number of conceivable choices raises the level of complexity. We have entered a period of turbulence in which no signs of future stability are in sight.

Although there is clearly no magic formula for dealing with all these issues, we *can* adopt a general outlook that will make the task easier. Today, we need to take a close look at our all too narrow view of capitalism and try to determine what is worth saving, what is worth transforming, and what is worth discarding entirely.

We are living under the tyranny of
quantitative performance.

The weight of economic considerations and the dogma of quantitative performance have nearly cancelled out all other concerns. This limited aspect of the world comes blaring out of all the loudspeakers today, while other, more disturbing sounds that people would rather not hear are barely audible. Since the collapse of communism in the East, a triumphant, free-market world view has been rapidly gaining ground. With relentless logic and arrogance, it aims at establishing itself throughout the world.

Now that the somewhat vague concept of globalization is in fashion, nation-states and their leaders are desperately trying to figure out how to react to a new situation that often leaves them confused. Both their uncertainty as to what their function should be and the complexity of today's environment prevent them from seeing clearly.

To explain this new powerlessness of our society's leaders, it is sometimes asserted that the pyramid of authority has been turned upside down. For those of us working in the business world, this boils down to the basic fact that the consumers are now the ones who hold the awesome power to make or break a business proposition. A similar trend can be observed in the field of politics, with politicians following the voters and keeping an eye on the opinion polls. The kings and leaders who ruled with sovereign power are a thing of the past. Whether we like it or not, this is the way things now are.

Millions of increasingly educated young people manifest a desire to express themselves, to choose their own future, but their aspirations come up against the resistance of the older generation, which claims to offer them rational, tried and tested solutions.

Yet in a world in which knowledge is developing and circulating with great speed, there is no turning the clock back. At present, millions of people come out into the streets every time they glimpse a chance to shape their own destiny, as in Rumania and Bulgaria. In this volatile political context, the irruption of mass movements propels journalists, writers, and professors into decision-making positions, instead of government officials and industrialists.

Our society didn't work that way in the past. In Europe (and in fact, as Dumézil has shown, throughout the Indo-European world), society was divided up into a hierarchy of three orders: the clergy, the nobility, and the third estate. In India as well, the Brahmans stood at the top of the ladder, followed by the warriors, while the merchant cast accepted a lower rung. Lastly, all the way at the bottom, were the untouchables, the cast from which India's latest president comes.

Times have changed, of course. Misuse of power ultimately caused these traditional systems to fall apart. It should be recalled, however, that in the early stages of our civilization, spiritual power was always located above temporal power. Kings were crowned by the highest ecclesiastic authorities.

During a talk he gave to a forum of leading businesspeople, French philosopher André Comte-Sponville asked his audience what order could foster an ethical, harmonious society.[1]

Certainly not the techno-scientific order, he said, nor the spontaneous functioning of the economy, both of which put all facts on par, without making value judgments.

Scientific laws distinguish between truth and falsehood, not between right and wrong. There exist no valid scientific reasons for holding back scientific progress. The only possible form of regulation must be moral.

Likewise, there are no economic grounds for limiting the interplay of economic forces. The famous laws of the free market led to widespread use of child labor, a practice to which society can hardly resign itself.

Yet the democratic order–whether seen in juridical or political terms–is equally powerless to control these areas of life. After all, Hitler came to power by legal means. Countries might very well vote democratically to institute eugenic measures or perpetrate genocide. To be sure, morality, which spells out duties and prohibitions, has an influence on the Constitution, but the Constitution can always be amended.

Only a higher, ethical order based on love requires no limits. It alone can guarantee the regulation of all the other orders.

To be perfectly realistic, we have a long way to go before ethics take precedence over economics. And however much we may regret the predominance of economic concerns, it happens to be the way of the world.

> *The function of competitive intelligence is to*
> *help us create events instead of just reacting them.*

We can no longer afford to base our thinking on past experience, or even to extrapolate from the present, in order to foresee the future. The current upheaval, as exemplified by globalization of the economy, compels us to go beyond mere reaction and to adopt a proactive stance.

Being proactive is the opposite of confining yourself to a defensive position. It means determining your future, actively creating events instead of being affected by them.

The notion of proactivity is indissociable from the main theme of this book. In this light, we feel confident enough to assert that *com-*

---

1. "Sur quoi fonder l'éthique?" André Comte-Sponville's opinion can be found in Robert Salmon, *The Future of Management. All Roads Lead to Man* (Blackwell, 1996), p. 103-104.

petitive intelligence has become a vital function in today's business world.

Although competitive intelligence may be viewed as a practical program, it would be more accurate to consider it a totally new approach to management.

Some observers have defined it as intelligent management of information, centered on a wise use of data regarding rival firms. To our way of thinking, however, something far richer, far more ambitious is involved. Competitive intelligence should be seen as a new cognitive map, a powerful tool that helps companies to take their place in the coming era and provides them with a new frame of mind that is in keeping with the trends currently emerging in our environment.

Agility, vision, scanning activity, and knowledge management are the interlocking themes in the concept of competitive intelligence.

For the time being, competitive intelligence remains a rather uncommon approach that has yet to win widespread recognition. Lacking a long-range vision, many firms continue to focus on the short term. And all too often, competitive intelligence is assumed to be a mere extension of the hard-core methods used in military and strategic intelligence. In the business world, this notion invariably brings to mind the idea of industrial espionage.

At this stage, we must stress a crucial point. *Competitive intelligence has nothing in common with reprehensible practices like spying and stealing industrial secrets.* It is much more a matter of hunting down information, an effort that is both entirely legitimate and vital to business success.

> *The "intelligence" required for making sound decisions has to cover a wide variety of areas.*

In business as well as in politics, "intelligence" gives decision-makers the elements they need to clarify their mid-range and long-term policies. In the context of a company, it helps managers to make the right decisions.

We would be sorely mistaken to imagine that in today's environment, all that firms need to achieve success is proper management. Technological change is profoundly modifying every aspect of the business environment, inevitably creating a growing number of dangers.

To be effective, competitive intelligence has to be practiced by multidisciplinary teams capable of keeping up on a wide range of areas. The research—and the introspection—that it entails should extend to cover many horizons, including society, technology, economy, environment, and even politics. The people in charge of competitive intelligence must therefore be able to conduct subtle analysis on local situations, but within the extremely broad framework of the global environment.

Furthermore, this activity cannot be carried out in sporadic fashion. It must continually monitor the firm's various business areas, providing them with the ongoing support they need to keep step with the competition. Competitive intelligence is a long-range undertaking–a kind of perpetual capacity for reaction.

> *In a largely unregulated world, the corporation is as yet the only truly global institution.*

As we have seen, competitive intelligence is essential for companies to achieve lasting success. But it also reflects the need for thorough questioning of dominant economic models and greater awareness of the role companies can play in developing new ways of doing things. The corporation has emerged as a world-wide player, undoubtedly the only truly global decision-making structure.

In a world where public regulation is often weak or inefficient, we can detect a new tendency for companies to assume a certain regulatory function. Current discussions on the social responsibility of corporations, the emergence of more sophisticated forms of lobbying, and the tendency of powerful multinationals to apply ecological standards all attest to growing awareness on the part of companies of the role they can now play.

> *From East to West, from Asia to Africa, there are major sources of uncertainty everywhere.*

In this regard, the international economic configuration should be taken into account. The world economic framework, i.e. the way in which influence is distributed, has never stood on such shaky, crumbling, shifting ground as it now does. Let's consider the broad outlines of the current world situation.

• *While the East is groping its way between a disappointing market economy and its initiation to political freedom, the West is having trouble reconciling affluence, growth, and ethics.*

Europe today is suffering from an extremely morose climate. The entire continent seems to have slid into a lasting slump. Nor are the coming years likely to wipe out the legacy of mass unemployment, social injustice, and political corruption, all of which are symptomatic of the recession that has been plaguing Europe for some time now. The laborious construction of the European Union is happening essentially by default, in the absence of any clear-cut support from public opinion.

• *The economic miracles in the Far East have lost much of their miraculous character, perhaps even to the point of grinding to a halt.* [1]

---

1. *Translator's note:* it should be borne in mind that these prophetic lines were written in 1996, i.e. well before the onset of the current crisis in the region.

The Japanese economy can no longer boast of exceptional buoyancy or superior strength.

Likewise, the miracle of the famous "dragons" appears to be petering out. In all likelihood, these countries will soon bear a strong resemblance to the Western nations, gradually adopting the norms of the developed world.

• *A whole series of unknowns raises doubts as to whether there is hope for further development in the world.*

The Islamic countries are confronted with the fundamentalist threat.

For the time being, Black Africa is out of the running, but what the situation will be like in fifty years is anybody's guess.

As for the two emerging great powers, China and India, they must strive to achieve an acceptable balance between their potential for economic growth and the weight of age-old traditions that often stand in the way of development.

Only North and South America seem to be blessed with lastingly favorable economic perspectives, in spite of a whole host of alarming problems such as the rising percentage of the population living below the poverty line and skyrocketing crime rates.

Still, however depressing the outlook may seem, the leading world economic indicators turn out–surprisingly enough–to be rather encouraging.

EXAMPLE

■ ECONOMIC FORECASTS FOR **1997** indicate a reasonable growth rate, although fairly modest in some areas. Thus, while the United States has clearly entered a boom that may keep the dollar from rising further, projected growth rates are 2% for all of the OECD countries, 2.5% for continental Europe, 8% for Asia as a whole, 10% for China, 4% for Latin America and Eastern Europe, and 5% for Africa. Russia is the only region with a steadily declining economic situation.

• *How does France fare in this rough sketch of the world economic situation?*

Although one of the wealthiest countries in the world, France is going through a highly disconcerting period. Apparently incapable of reducing the jobless rate, the nation's political leaders seem to be plodding along with the same old threadbare social-democratic recipes–or what is left of them. Meanwhile, the judiciary is struggling to assert its authority, the rural population is massively leaving the countryside, only to swell the ranks of the urban unemployed, the poor, and even the homeless.

If the people governing the country continue onward in the same direction, without proposing any broader vision or "reason to believe", France will drag its accumulated doubts, fears, rigidities, and sterile forms of selfish behavior well into the twenty-first century. The British already call the French *les misérables*, in reference to Victor Hugo's famous novel, while the American press rarely misses an opportunity to present skeptical analyses of French society and politics.

One wonders how France can continue to be the scene of such paradoxes, given its fabulous assets, including world-class corporations, leading-edge technology, and artistic achievement.

Our future depends on what we do. From here on in, one key word ought to guide us in our business activity–hope. With the means now available to us, we should be able to push this proactive mind-set much further and leave behind the passive, gloomy mentality so common today.

We businesspeople have an important part to play.

This is where we businesspeople come in. We have a huge, destabilizing, but nonetheless vital part to play.

Today's companies are increasingly exposed to heavy international competition. Yet many of them are adapting, working hard to understand the new business environment. There is by now an impressive list of success stories and encouraging experiments that can provide us with valuable insights in such a difficult context.

A growing number of firms are now keenly aware of the *global environment*. They sense how crucial it is to pay close attention to the people around them, to their competitors, and to the social setting in which they operate.

Our aim must be to develop a vision that steers clear of all forms of dogmatism. To do so, we need a specific approach of the kind that competitive intelligence has to offer. This concept is taking firm root in successful companies that intend to stay successful. It is often the major American corporations that have broken new ground in this area.

A trend should not be equated with blind fate. It isn't premeditated, but it isn't a matter of pure chance, either. A trend reflects a particular pattern. It is up to us to find the proper frame of reference for working out pragmatic strategies.

Performance cannot be our ultimate goal.

We must emphasize, however, that the frantic race for ever-improved performance cannot be our ultimate goal. Although long-term health is a prerequisite to any company's survival, it isn't the be-all and end-all of business activity. We also need to find a subtle combination between economic criteria and other, less tangible factors.

In recent years, economic considerations have succeeded to an alarming degree in pushing aside all other concerns. If nothing is done to reverse this trend, we may wake up one day to find ourselves in an inhuman, unliveable world.

By judging a society solely on the basis of its financial achievements, we tend, albeit unwittingly, to foster forms of behavior that run counter to harmonious human relations. The pursuit of rising profits at any cost fails to take people into account, although people now constitute the main competitive resource of any company.

A firm can only achieve lasting success if it mobilizes the energy of everyone involved and a leader or management team manages to convey a sense of belonging, to channel the vital forces in the right direction, and thereby to create a corporate vision that has meaning for all.

Today's companies must relentlessly struggle to imagine, develop, and implement solutions that take their inspiration from the new key factors in business. What we mean are those intangible elements that go beyond mere economic values, and above all, people.

GROWTH: A LASTING IMPERATIVE

Let's start out with a simple observation. Competitive intelligence goes hand in hand with a particular kind of company, the kind that never loses sight of the absolute need to grow.

> *We businesspeople are now keenly aware*
> *of just how mortal we are.*

Our traditional management methods were predicated on the idea of unchanging, immortal companies. In fact, however, companies are born and die at a much higher rate than we generally imagine, in just two or three generations. Some giants of the business world sink into a process of irreversible decline, a phenomenon that is bound to intensify in the future. Neither the glorious record nor the much-vaunted corporate culture of these companies will save them. The list of once famous firms that have been swallowed up by others includes Chevrolet, Simca, Talbot, and Gervais. The relevant questions are, of course, why, and whether there is some way of escaping such a fate.

The future no longer belongs to General Motors, but to Microsoft. Government intervention in the economy is nothing but a rear-guard struggle. Using various life-support systems to keep giants with clay feet alive only slows down the emergence of new, dynamic, enterprising firms.

No company is immortal. Most of the ones that currently appear to be didn't even exist when our grandparents were around. Of the 100 American firms located at the top of the "Fortune 500" in 1970, only 29 are still there today.

Foreign companies have fared no better, with only 27 of them maintaining their superior position. As for the usual heavyweights–General Motors, Ford, and IBM–although they continue to occupy three of the top four positions in terms of sales, they have lost considerable ground with respect to profits.

The conclusion to be drawn from these figures is that in the course of an average working life, roughly two thirds of the world's leading companies have been outstripped by faster developing rivals.

You can't help wondering how firms at the height of their glory can pay so little attention to their environment and to the progress their competitors are making that they wake up one day to find that they have been left behind. Some lose their leading position and get bought out by more successful companies, while others turn into technological dinosaurs.

The sad truth is that history plays only a minor role in business. However remarkable a company's record may be, its future is determined above all by how full its order books will be in the coming months–or even weeks. All its takes is for the company to lower its guard momentarily. In the long run, a solid reputation is no protection against sudden jolts.

EXAMPLES

■ **AS LONG AS THE IRRESISTIBLE RISE OF DIGITAL EQUIPMENT (DEC)** was still a reality, no one would have dreamt that the company would disappear. After all, CEO Ken Olsen was the one who invented the mini-computer, a more streamlined version of the office computer. Building a veritable empire on this innovation, DEC became a model, a company deeply imbued with a humanistic vision of management and capable of organizing along radically new lines. On the basis of independent profit centers, DEC set up a highly efficient system of customer relations that resembled an upside-down pyramid.

DEC probably derived a feeling of infallibility from its phenomenal success. As a result, the company initiated a costly project: Rainbow, a product that was clearly both unusual and out of sync with market trends at a time in which Hewlett Packard was developing its RISK architecture with the help of Unix, whose choice of open systems was to prove much more promising.

The interesting thing about this example is that Ken Olsen had already anticipated the trend toward smaller, easier to handle computers.

In 1987, DEC was the world's number two computer company, with a workforce of 110,000. Ever since, it has been steadily declining. Although the inventor of the mini, it failed to anticipate and therefore missed the shift toward the PC, with its universally accepted standards. Even so, it looks as though it might be able to bounce back again, owing to its new Alpha architecture and its agreements with Microsoft.

■ **RANK XEROX,** which used to dominate the photocopy market, producing four out of five copy machines sold in the world in 1976, suffered a dramatic drop in market share to a mere 13% in 1982. The company's leaders were convinced that the lower price at which their Japanese competitors sold their machines was a sign of inferior quality. They were wrong, and underestimating their rival Ricoh cost Xerox its previously unchallenged leadership in the business.

■ **WITH COMPETITION FROM INTERNET, CD** sales may take such a beating that sooner or later, the principle of the "megastore" like Virgin will undoubtedly require some serious rethinking.

This explains why our vision of the future is constantly subordinated to current economic trends, including unexpected events, the growing importance of the monetary factor, and intensified competition. The short term has become so crucial that we have a hard time simply seeing beyond it.

> *In times of crisis, companies certainly react,*
> *but their reactions may not be appropriate.*

For a number of years now, large corporations around the world have been reorganizing various aspects of their business. In order to cut costs, they practice downsizing and outsourcing, or they jump onto the famous reengineering bandwagon. Yet if one thing stands out starkly today, it is that these efforts rarely seem to bring about any significant, lasting improvement.

In point of fact, companies are not suffering from overabundant production factors, but rather from a basic, structural problem of competitive strength that tends to push down their profit margins.

> *New management styles should be taken with a grain of salt.*

In management as elsewhere, fashion plays a role. There was a time in which the theory of leading "gurus" aimed at concentrating knowledge in the hands of top managers. At present, however, it appears to be impossible to give full control of extremely complex processes to a single person. Taylorism has seen its day.

Recognition of this shift has given rise to new styles of management, including TQM, reengineering, "lean management," and "time-based management"(cf. graph).

MANAGMENT CONCEPTS BROUGHT INTO FASHION
BY CONSULTANTS BETWEEN 1950 AND 1995

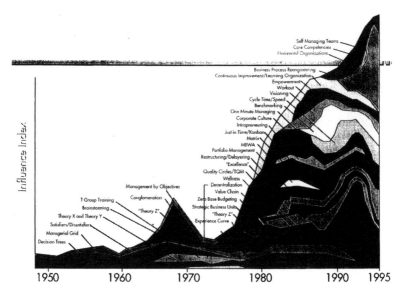

Graph presented by Richard Pascale during a talk given in Brussels in 1995.

MANAGEMENT CONCEPTS BROUGHT INTO FASHION
BY CONSULTANTS BETWEEN 1950 AND 1995

Period	Management Concepts
1950-1960	Decision trees Managerial Grid
1960-1970	Satisfiers/Dissatisfiers Theory X and Theory Y
1970-1980	Brainstorming T-Group Training Conglomeration Management by Objectives Decentralization Experience Curve
1980-1990	Theory Z Strategic Business Units Zero-Base Budgeting Value Chain Wellness Quality Circles/TQM "Excellence" Restructuring/Delayering Portfolio Management MBWA Matrix Just-in-time/Kanban Intrapreneuring Corporate Culture One-Minute Managing Benchmarking Cycle Time/Speed Visioning Workout Empowerment Continuous Improvement/Learning Organization
1990-1995	Business Process Reengineering Horizontal Organizations Core Competencies Self-Managing Teams

All these models are, of course, based on the premise that the stream of Taylorism has run dry. They were conceived as a means to adjust to a changing world. The important point, however, is to take things further and find out exactly why the world is changing so fast.

Our civilization now celebrates Results, enthusiastically taking up virtually any concept that starts out with the magic syllable "re", such as reform, restructure, revise, rethink, revamp, not to mention the most revered "re" of all–reengineer. The Egyptian sun god Ra has apparently been replaced by the god Re. Unfortunately, however, neither all these "re"'s nor time-based management offer sufficient means for dealing with the continuous change we are experiencing. Anyone who attempts to catch up faster and faster is likely to get dizzy.

| The god Ra | The god Re |

Growth: Both an Obligation and an Ambition

Growth as the Starting Point for a Virtuous Circle

Growth can send out good vibrations of a special kind, creating a congenial atmosphere in companies, stimulating investment, and encouraging talent.

Growth is thus the source that feeds a virtuous circle. It stimulates and reassures workers, which is crucial in periods of intense research and creativity. It also attracts investors, thus strengthening the company's competitive position.

*In a depressed climate or in a languishing
company, creativity tends to decline
dramatically.*

Without growth, we have no way of attracting talent, developing it,
gaining the loyalty of those who possess it, stimulating it, or realizing
its creative potential. It is vital today to reverse the tendency of all too
many executives to devote a large part of their time to essentially
uncreative tasks.

**THE DIMINISHING PERCENTAGE OF WORK TIME DEVOTED
TO CREATIVE TASKS***

	1980		1988		1996 (extrapolation)	
	Reactive	**Creative**	**Reactive**	**Creative**	**Reactive**	**Creative**
Employees	90%	10%	93%	7%	95%	5%
Executives	48%	52%	63%	37%	70-80%	20-30%

* Based on a point made in R. Larson and David Zimney, eds., *White Collar Shuffle*,
Amacom, 1990.

Maintaining an Ambition for Growth

*Winners know that growth is something they
achieve through their own efforts.*

To maintain a growth perspective, we have to take control of our
fate. The companies that do 15% better are the ones that truly believe
in themselves.

Although growth is a variable, it should be considered an internal,
rather than an external one. All necessary growth comes from within.

*The desire to move faster than the market is
conducive to fruitful questioning about how
things are done.*

Philips, Nike, Unilever, and L'Oréal are companies that daily demonstrate their will to stay on top. That means regarding growth as an
inescapable imperative.

Some companies succeed in significantly increasing both sales and
profits, while others regress.

If we content ourselves with progressing at the same rate as the
market, we won't be able to muster enough courage to submit to the
painful, but necessary soul-searching. In contrast, as soon as we fix

highly ambitious, double-digit growth objectives, we realize that we can't achieve them with conventional methods. We know that the time has come to start reconsidering the company's processes and its entire value chain.

EXAMPLE

■ **THE URGE FOR EXCELLENCE** can be seen in the slogans of several companies. "Just do it," at Nike, "Let's make things better," at Philips, "Leader or number 2 in each of our segments," at Unilever, "A constantly renewed technological promise," at L'Oréal, "I dreamed it, Sony did it," at Sony.

The will to grow may sound like wishful thinking, but only a spirit of conquest, combined with solid managerial sense, provides the stimuli that forge winning teams. A company has to be aware of its value and of the assets that enable it to rank with the best.

Three Lethal Potions: Crisis, Doubt–and Success

In an environment of crisis and uncertainty, a conquering attitude is by no means self-evident. It has to overcome the economic climate, managerial inertia, distorted perceptions regarding business areas, erroneous views on growth strategies, as well as ingrained pessimism and short-sightedness. The most dangerous obstacles are probably of a cultural nature, meaning that they are internal to the company.

The Economic Doldrums of the Headquarters Country

The country in which corporate headquarters are located may influence the company's performance in various ways. In a country suffering from openly depressed conditions, even though the global economy is, on the whole, doing fairly well, the company may find itself drawn into the sluggish local climate, thereby suffering a loss of dynamism.

EXAMPLE

■ **FOR SEVERAL YEARS NOW,** Japanese companies seem to have lost a good deal of their former momentum. The general economic climate in the Land of the Rising Sun is undoubtedly one of the factors explaining this trend.

When GDP and average consumption begin to look stagnant, companies have a hard time forecasting buoyantly optimistic results. Yet there is every reason to assume that whatever its line of business, the country in which it operates, and the stage of development it has reached, a company always possesses a certain potential for growth.

Culture, Organization, Business and Product Evaluation as Possible Dampers

The main obstacles to dynamic growth often lie in the surrounding culture, the rigidity of organizations, the systems of compensation used, or the way in which different lines of business are perceived within the firm. They stem from the existence of management styles that are ill-suited to the company's dynamic capabilities.

Such obstacles may also reflect a lack of strategic daring, which prevents the company's leaders from analyzing the value of their product and service portfolio in relation to the services and cost structure of their competitors. Thus, year after year, the same old budget gets voted. In contrast, if you truly absorb what you have learned from the competition and give fresh thought to the nature of your product and service portfolio, you often discover new, unsuspected opportunities.

Further obstacles result from mistakes made in defining growth strategies. Companies that are accustomed to success tend to construct rigid models out of their achievements and to continue to apply them, even when the environment has shifted. This is a natural phenomenon involving the way in which beliefs take root. What we consider a recipe for success turns out to be little more than a disturbing penchant for smug self-satisfaction.

The Success Trap

A company's success already contains the seeds of possible decline. Maintaining what has worked so far is a common human trait. Unfortunately, however, the recipes that helped you succeed yesterday may not prove to be as useful tomorrow.

> *The culture of success sometimes manifests*
> *itself in arrogance and in a sense of infallibility*
> *that contribute toward killing off healthy*
> *alertness and the willingness to take risks.*

Success creates an internal culture that turns out to be difficult to call into question. In lines of business that depend greatly on technological innovation, companies must be able to adjust to sudden quantum leaps in technology, but their leaders are often emotionally attached to their products. They see no grounds for changing a winning team or a fast-selling product.

■ STATING THAT "IBM IS NOT IN THE TOY BUSINESS," the company's leaders refused to believe in the future of the PC, a monitor they judged far too lacking in power to be taken seriously. Blinded by this basic assumption, they failed to perceive the advent of the software era. As a result, IBM soon took a beating from its competitors, to such an extent that it forfeited its former leading position.

■ IN THE MOBILE TELEPHONE BATTLE, MOTOROLA showed a lack of competitive intelligence. Because it didn't develop the necessary chips in time, it missed its chance to enter the digital age.

Success often breeds arrogance as well. Managers of leading companies convince themselves that they owe it all to their own competence. In such a case, the company's competitive advantage is threatened by a feeling of infallibility that keeps it from tuning in to the weak signals in the environment that foreshadow significant new trends.

The fact of the matter is that market leaders are psychologically less able to take advantage of technological change, since they feel a basic urge to hold such change back, whereas their competitors make full use of the new technologies to launch their attack.

■ IN SPITE OF THEIR PHENOMENAL SUCCESS in the late nineteenth century, the railroad companies proved incapable of inventing the aeronautical industry. There are countless other examples of companies enjoying such unchallenged supremacy in their field that they underestimated major technological shifts, from jet planes to phonograph records and quartz watches. They thereby fell behind and never caught up again.

Simply coasting along on past achievements makes managers reluctant to question their approach. Proper management of success means cultivating distrust.

Top management is often more concerned with conserving existing structures than with mapping out the required changes. Thus, some businesses may well go into an imperceptible, yet inexorable decline, while still achieving apparently respectable results. Maximum profits cannot protect mature firms from succumbing to inertia.

In such cases, managers merely coast along on past achievements rather than imagining new ways to pick up speed. Large Western corporations, with their cohorts of managers and analysts, are past masters in this art, which consists of making sure at all times that no one can find fault with your work.

The Need to Branch Off in Time

The idea of branching off, which the Nobel prize-winning chemist Ilia Prigogine likes to stress, leads to a transformation in thinking that helps companies reinvent their future. Like so many other low-amplitude phenomena that generate massive breaks, it should not be underestimated.

All companies go through an inevitable evolutionary process that leads through various phases of growth. They are born, they develop, and then they reach maturity, a stage at which the perspective of decline looms up. Analysis of the famous "Sigmoid Curve," which describes the life cycle of a company, underscores the need to manage branching off in order to pave the way for a different future. Every company must make sure to start down the second loop in time so it can begin a new cycle. If it misses the turn, it is already on the road to decline, without even noticing it, particularly since it may still be chalking up stunning achievements.

As soon as success becomes a self-perpetuating phenomenon, a healthy anxiety should take hold of the company.

Any company leader who aims at setting out along a new "Sigmoid Curve" must have a clear idea of the distinction between past accomplishments and factors of progress like innovation and creativity.

The Three Phases of the "Sigmoid Curve"

Phase 1: FORGING AHEAD (motivation, enthusiasm, experimentation)

The company undergoes a period of intensive creativity. It invents its own future. In this phase that is to constitute the company's memory, conventional management methods are discarded. The main point is being inventive, flexible, and bold—even reckless.

In this first phase, vigorous growth is almost always due to a solid competitive advantage that makes the company particularly popular with consumers. Outstanding performance tends to go hand in hand with carefully controlled costs, which are often lower than the costs of competitors, since the firm is still relatively modest in scope.

This entrepreneurial stage is an imaginative one in which people have the courage to improvise and to stray from the usual paths followed in that particular line of business. Imbued with fear of failure and the will to survive, the teams involved carry out this experimental work in a festive, euphoric atmosphere. The company's employees see themselves almost as missionaries of a new religion, preaching unshakeable faith in their product or service.

Over and over again, the ingenious, unpredictable side of this trial and error period produces both feelings of victory and intense frustration. At this stage, there is no point in benchmarking, since instinct and improvisation are the key ingredients. As in a jam session, there is a good groove, and although no one knows exactly how it is that the players are so attuned to each other, everyone senses that the sound is right.

THE SIGMOID CURVE

"The secret of constant growth is to start a new Sigmoid curve before the first one peters out. The right place to start that second curve is at point A, where there is the time, as well as the resources and the energy, to get the new curve through its initial explorations and flounderings before the first curve begins to dip downwards.

"That would seem obvious; were it not for the fact that at point A all the messages coming through to the individual or the institution are that everything is going fine, that it would be folly to change when the current recipes are working so well. All that we know of change, be it personal change or change in organizations, tells us that the real energy for change only comes when you are looking disaster in the face at point B on the first curve...

"Wise are they who start the second curve at point A, because that is the Pathway through Paradox, the way to build a new future while maintaining the present." [1]

---

1. Charles Handy, *The Empty Raincoat* (Hutchinson, London, 1994), p. 51-52.

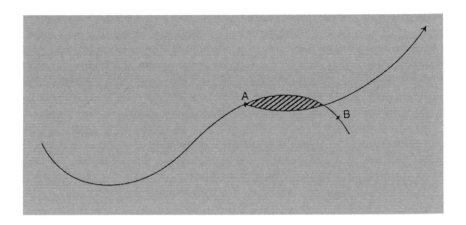

Phase 2: HARNESSING (managing, codifying, laying down rules)

At this stage, the company attempts to implement rules, procedures, and methods in order to reproduce, develop, and improve
upon the elements responsible for its initial success, or to avoid
repeating the mistakes that were inevitably made along the way.

The dominant attitude seems to be the desire to do away with the
unpredictable, to introduce rigid management techniques aimed at
guaranteeing the firm's long-term survival. After a period of bold,
wilful conquest, a retreat into caution occurs. Management is now a
matter of strictly enforced rules and procedures, of quantitative measures, as creativity gets the short end of the stick. The well-known
Wall Street syndrome—"short-termism"—sets in, with managers
sometimes going to absurd lengths to maximize profits.

Everyone is nonetheless convinced that the company is engaged
in a useful process of codifying the patterns that ensured its prior
success, of extending and consolidating its achievements. Thus, at
the first sign of adversity, a convenient response is to blame someone
else. We all remember the hue and cry over Far Eastern dumping
practices.

Phase 3: CONFRONTING (or not)

At this point, the company would do well to set up special units
for monitoring the overall situation, if it hasn't already done so at the
preceding stage, since it now finds itself faced with rapidly rising
complexity, both inside the organization and on its markets.

Globalization leads to the proliferation of competitive product
offers, in a context of increasing market fragmentation. In such a
situation, internal rivalry over resource allocation tends to heat up.

If the company hasn't carried out the necessary soul-searching, all
these managerial shortcomings can bring about lower profit margins,

shrinking market share, and stagnant productivity, precisely at a time when technological breakthroughs make it more necessary than ever to invest heavily in order to avoid being outstripped by competitors. In such a case, the company is ripe for decline. It can, however, turn the situation entirely around, provided that its CEO is able to give the firm a powerful impulse toward change. A prime example is Jack Welch, who succeeded in breathing new life into all of General Electric's lines of business by systematically shaking up the usual patterns of work.

Between Magic Potions and Blind Faith

Taking a Middle Course Between Stress and Complacency

What is often lacking is a tool, a mind-set that helps companies seize the time.

Running a company is a highly demanding art. The CEO is constantly torn between the absolute need for growth, the risk of becoming complacent as a result of success, and the importance of breaking conventional patterns of thinking.

Only by maintaining a creative thrust strong enough to avoid both stress and complacency can a company grow, and thus develop that sense of pride and belonging that gives it the necessary dynamism. No growth means no jobs.

Only by turning resolutely toward the future can we open up new vistas that ensure the ongoing development of both the company and the community it forms.

> *Even if excessive constraints lead to skepticism,*
> *we still must believe in growth.*

Winning firms–the ones that seem to manage to maintain high growth figures and to remain in the forefront of new developments, however difficult the business climate may be–undoubtedly have one point in common that cannot be sufficiently stressed. They have always wanted to come out on top, and they have always considered it possible to do so.

Yet although such leading companies constantly give top priority to growth, they tend to be hampered in their desire to develop internally, and even externally, by a long list of difficulties and constraints, including recession in Europe, the problem of breaking into new, unfamiliar markets, the sluggishness of mature markets, declining product differentiation, and the tremendous downward pressure on profits, often accentuated by rising costs.[1]

In light of the rather uninspiring outlook in Europe (which still is the main market for most European companies), company leaders have trouble planning for high rates of growth. It often appears that their awareness of multiple constraints has gradually worn down their confidence in growth, which was formerly easier to achieve. As a result, a good many companies suspend their bold plans for expansion, opting instead for various solutions that involve rationalization, downsizing, or even disinvestment, whose harmful effects are by now so evident that there is no need to belabor the point.

> *Stringent management policies cannot bring about significant improvements in the situation of companies.*

The policies just mentioned generate a number of negative consequences:
- The image of the company as a social institution deteriorates.
- Productivity suffers from the law of diminishing returns.
- The company is still insufficiently competitive, unless it decides to do a large part of its production offshore, in low-wage countries.

Furthermore, profit margins no longer grow in today's depressed economic climate, in which customers seek low-cost products, while demanding a wide variety of goods and services.

Lastly, the image of many products suffers, as customers gradually turn away from companies made infamous by their downsizing practices. This is what happened to Hoover, and more recently to Renault, in Belgium. In the United States, consumers appear to be fed up with companies they consider inhuman for continuing to reduce their workforce even when the economy appears to be picking up.[2]

This leads to the question as to what the new sources of growth will be, those that could breathe new life into the system.

Emerging Markets: Beware of Mirages

The apparent obstacles to growth on traditional markets have strengthened the temptation to branch out into the emerging markets, especially in Asia, at high investment cost.

However, companies that do little more than shift their dreams of expansion elsewhere are most likely on the wrong track. It certainly is

---

1. Source: Boston Consulting Group.
2. Cf. "L'Amérique réinvente l'entreprise", *L'Expansion,* Oct. 24, 1996.

possible to find new, high-growth markets, in Asia, for example, but such a strategy entails considerable initial investments. The more sustained growth achieved on such markets proves to be unable to compensate for poor results on traditional markets. The reason for this is that although sales often progress by leaps and bounds on this "New Frontier," profit margins continue at the same time to decline on mature markets. Companies following such a strategy may well find themselves in a highly precarious position.

> *Elsewhere and later can never replace here and now.*

It would be foolish for companies to give up on their home markets. They should view growth as a constant obligation, to be extended to all regions and all lines of business in which they operate. This is the only way to gain and keep a competitive edge.

It isn't enough to be in the right place at the right time; you also have to be in the forefront. When skillfully managed, competitive intelligence can make for well-balanced corporate performance. But however necessary competitiveness may be in today's business world, it isn't enough.

Competitive intelligence can help us avoid the pitfalls of obsessive focus on achieving competitive strength. Such a focus often generates unexpected and undesirable effects like low motivation, dwindling creativity, and, in the long run, a lack of new projects, which spells company decline.

THE START OF THE DOWNSIZING WAVE (% OF WORKFORCE, 1983)*

5-10% Decrease		Over 10% Decrease	
BASF	8	J. E. Seagram	17
Data General	8	Owen-Illinois	16
Westinghouse		Monsanto	11
Borden	6	Union Carbide	13
Dressert	5		
IBM	13		
Bethlehem Steel	7	Digital	17
General Motors	5	Amdahl	30
Honeywell	6	Kodak	17

* 1983 saw the onset of large-scale downsizing in the United States, a movement still under way today. We have limited this table to operations carried out in that one year (including staff reductions resulting from sales of assets) to avoid opening up more recent wounds. (Source: "The Fortune 500," *Fortune*, April 18, 1994.)

Taming the Urge for Competitive Advantage

The desire for growth should not induce companies to seek competitive advantage at any cost. Managing change must not become synonymous with putting the company in jeopardy.

The profile of companies has undergone considerable evolution over the past several years. The meaning of work has been reconsidered in our society, corporations have cut back their staff, and their organizational structures have been flattened out, thus opening the way to rising productivity in many areas.

How far should we take such competitive restructuring?

Reengineering operations often reduce personnel by as much as 50%. On the basis of totally unattainable objectives, the notion of Total Quality Management (TQM) has become a convenient excuse for cutting back or exploiting the workforce.

Current business discussion must focus on the human factor, because in any company, people are the main source of competitive advantage and the key to success. Only those companies that ask the right questions about their aims, their role in the community, their ethical dimension, and their responsibility to society will be able to come up with the winning combination, and thus to survive.

Nations or Companies: Is the Competitive Race Inescapable?

Over the last two decades, the unprecedented development of systems that interconnect markets around the world has made the different economies profoundly interdependent. The resulting shifts in activity from country to country blur traditional borders and categories, sometimes even leading to inappropriate adjustments.

There is no shortage today of advisory boards on how to achieve competitive advantage. Nations now engage in "competition over competitiveness." This has greatly increased the level of stress and destabilized the labor market, as jobs becoming precarious and wages are held in check.

You can't help wondering whether there isn't a breaking point beyond which any further striving for greater efficiency might threaten the very survival of companies and even entire nations.

Both ecological constraints and the social repercussions of economic globalization will compel countries and companies to question their basic view of what progress is. Any major divergence between the global interests of transnational corporations and the interests of local workers and consumers may undermine the stability of consumer society.

THE WORLD'S FOUR POPULATIONS

The GBN [1] classification divides our planet up into four worlds: the affluent, the hopeful poor, the villagers, and the poor without hope.

The affluent world includes 300 million people who enjoy a high standard of living and who represent enormous market potential, as well as some 500 million others who make up the middle class, and who also achieve high levels of consumption.

The category of the hopeful poor includes the 800 million people located just below middle-class status. Moving steadily upward, they live mainly in the strong economic development zones of Asia and Eastern Europe. Companies would be well advised to take an interest in this population segment, which will undoubtedly constitute the market of the future.

The villagers, some 2.5 million strong, live for the most part in Africa, as well as in certain regions of Latin America, the Middle East, and the Far East. Although not necessarily poor, these populations may nonetheless be viewed as disconnected from the modern world. As a consequence, the villagers will play no major role on the world market in the ten years to come.

In contrast, the poor without hope—about 1.2 million people—know that they are desperately poor and that they will probably remain so. They live in the shanty towns around the large South American cities, as well as in Africa, India, and Pakistan. In spite of their contact with consumer society, they have virtually no access to education, jobs, or new technology.

By the year 2020, global population should reach the 8.5 billion mark. 1.4 billion people will belong to the affluent world, 4.7 billion to the developing world, and 2.4 billion to the world of the forgotten, representing 28% of overall population. It is among these desperately poor that the various extremist currents will recruit revolutionaries and terrorists.

---

1. The Global Business Network, which includes 100 of the top companies in the world, is organized by Peter Schwartz, the former director of Group Planning at Shell, with the assistance of Napier Collyns and Gay Ogilvy, both of them former Shell collaborators.

If something isn't done about it, present-day society may well become a world of ruthless discrimination that seals off top economic performers from everyone else–the have-nots, the forgotten poor, the victims of progress.

Globalized, frenetic competition produces too many losers.

In situations of extreme competition, only those individuals and organizations achieving exceptional performance have a real chance of succeeding. This new phenomenon might be referred to as "the superstar syndrome." Those who excel get premium pay, the result being that the gap between rich and poor widens. Minor performance differentials now generate vast inequality in income.

Globalization proves to be a positive-sum game, one in which everyone gets richer, since it is the only way to share the benefits of growth. It thus represents hope for the future–except for those who get left out.

The dividing line will not run between rich countries and poor countries, because inequality between nations will probably lessen over time. Yet inequality within each nation may become more pronounced than before, with a group of winners opposed to a group of losers. If the losing population gets large enough, the whole process of globalization will break down, according to two possible scenarios. We will witness either a "soft" breakdown, with a gradual rise in protectionism everywhere, or a "hard" one, with much more serious consequences.

The crucial task is thus to avoid creating too many losers. Companies, however, may not be able to accomplish this on their own. Nation-states will have to recover their past importance, but in the context of new, more suitable systems to be developed. And although the World Trade Organization certainly represents a positive step, it is up to every country to prevent the emergence of large groups of outcasts on its soil.

A gigantic pool of potential desperadoes and terrorists.

Competitiveness must not be transformed into an absolute dogma that overshadows humanistic values. Managing change should not become synonymous with creating precarious conditions.

We have to be aware that if the number of people left out of the system increases beyond reasonable limits, the situation will become so uncontrollable and explosive that the entire frantic race now going on will be stopped. The number of poor without hope in the world has already reached the danger point. Some 700 million despairing young people are likely to contribute heavily to desperate, terrorist movements of all sorts. In any case, their numbers will continue to rise dramatically over the next fifteen years.

It has often been stressed that in today's open market environment, nations cannot afford to lower their competitive guard. The question we must now answer is whether they should meet this challenge, regardless of what it takes to do so.

> *For companies as well as for nations, economic success does not derive from isolated facts, but from a complex combination of factors that are usually internal.*

Many people tend to assume that opportunities for growth are generated above all by external factors that are ultimately beyond our control. In fact, however, more or less dynamic markets, the influence of competition, and the impact of new technology that may or may not be easy to master in short order should not be considered "free electrons" or forces to which we must submit.

It turns out that companies in a wide range of businesses (food processing, cosmetics, telecommunications, air travel) manage to maintain growth rates far higher than the average for their business, even in highly competitive markets.

Why are some firms so dynamic that they chalk up 15% increases in revenues, while others–the losers in the game–suffer a 15% decline? As we have already suggested, the trouble is that companies in the second category persist in considering the key factors external in one way or another. In all likelihood, the same holds true of nations. Analyzing their economic successes and failures is a subtle task that necessarily requires taking a large number of parameters into account.

For a nation, achieving economic strength is not merely a question of possessing one of the following assets.

• **Natural resources.** If this were the case, Zaire, South Africa, Iraq, and Algeria would rank among the most highly developed countries in the world.

• **Available capital.** Saudi Arabia was reported to have over 700 billion petro-dollars, but most of this colossal wealth was invested outside the country, on a private basis. Any industrialist will tell you that when a viable project is presented in an acceptable environment, obtaining the necessary financial backing is never a problem.

• **Intelligence.** Russia is one of the most advanced countries with regard to the concentration of mathematicians, scientists, engineers, and writers there. Likewise, Hungary has produced any number of Nobel Prize winners and unusually talented individuals (e.g. James Wolfensohn and George Soros). Yet neither of these two nations dominates the world.

• **Low costs, particularly labor costs.** If this were the decisive factor, the Sudan, Bangladesh, Angola, Ecuador, and Vietnam would be the most industrialized countries in the world.

What is required is a combination of all these assets, which must then be supplemented with the three following factors.

1. The country's belief in progress and the determination of its people.

2. A stable, duly enforced legal system.

3. A market economy with free trade. (The recipe for Far-Eastern growth, for example, does not derive essentially from Confucianism, but stems more prosaically from the high level of savings and investment, from the fact that private property is respected, and that state economic activity and public spending are kept to a minimum. We can certainly learn a good deal from such countries.)

> *Does the concept of competitiveness have any*
> *meaning when applied to nations in the same*
> *way as we apply it to companies?*

Although first applied to business, the concept of competitiveness has been extended to cover international relations as well. Every country is thus likened to "a giant company obliged to fight on the world market," as Bill Clinton once put it.

Yet the rivalry that exists between the world's leading nations cannot be equated with the business competition between multinational corporations. It is rather rivalry in terms of power and influence, which has little impact on the living standards of the populations involved.

The economic difficulties encountered by nations do not fundamentally result from a lack of effort on their part to conquer foreign markets. To be sure, the social and industrial system in some countries is better suited than others to the trend toward globalization and might thus well be considered more competitive. However, describing international relations in terms of competition would seem to be above all a way of pushing through unpopular policies, thereby attesting to a lack of political courage. A few observations should illustrate this contention.

Trade Between Nations is not a Zero-Sum Game

When Toyota increases its sales on the American market year after year, we might assume that General Motors' sales will suffer as a result. This line of reasoning, however, cannot be extended to nations. High growth rates in Europe should rather be a source of satisfaction for the United States, since it can expect to be able to boost its exports to Europe or to import higher-quality products at lower prices.

Countries Never Go Bankrupt

A company that is no longer competitive faces the prospect of getting wiped out of the market. Unable to pay its employees and its suppliers, it is in danger of going bankrupt.

Countries never experience such a dramatic situation, since they can stay on the map, however poor their economic performance may be. In the 1980s, Mexico looked upon its trade surplus as a sign of national weakness (restrictions had to be made in order to pay back the country's debt), whereas in the early 1990s, it viewed its trade deficit as a sign of force (once confidence was restored, foreign capital flowed in). Furthermore, what undermined confidence and generated an uncontrollable situation were intangible factors (the conflict in Chiapas, political assassination, etc.) rather than the level of Mexico's trade deficit (which hadn't gotten any worse).

The concept of "international competitiveness" thus proves to be meaningless when applied to nations, which are fundamentally different from companies.

A Country's Living Standards Mainly Reflect National Factors

We often hear definitions of "national competitiveness" as "the ability to produce goods and services that are competitive on the world market in order to offer our citizens steadily rising living standards." This formulation implies that the rise in a country's living standards is directly proportional to its trade volume.

It turns out, however, that this theory has never been tested in practice. Statistics from the U.S. Department of Commerce actually prove that the rise in living standards is of the same order of magnitude as growth in domestic productivity, rather than the productivity rate in relation to productivity rates abroad.

Even today, the United States exports a mere 10% of its GNP, meaning that 90% of the goods and services it produces go to the home market. Now we can see how absurd it is to compare nations with companies. If the comparison were valid, some companies would be selling 90% of their output to their own work force! Things have changed since Henry Ford was around. It is well known that today's leading multinationals sell next to nothing to their own workers.

> *The "competitive metaphor" is above all a rhetorical device used to mask economic failure.*

If the image of "countries fighting each other on world markets the way companies do" has enjoyed such popularity, it is because it strikes a familiar note and is easy to understand. Businessmen who are encouraged to view their country as if it were a firm get the impression that they have grasped the essential point.

In addition, images of warlike confrontation have an exciting flavor to them; they "sell" because they appear to be able to mobilize people. Unfortunately, they lead to overestimation of external factors, so much so that the internal reasons for carrying out necessary change become obscured.

If we believe that our economic difficulties stem basically from our inadequacies in international competition, we might hope to be able to straighten out the situation through short-term political measures (subsidies, devaluation, etc.) —which would give us the comforting feeling that our problems are easy to solve. In contrast, focusing on the national factors the stunt domestic productivity might well cause considerable concern. The reason for this is that there is not much hope for rapid improvement, since government policies have very little impact on most of the factors involved.

Political leaders have thus found a highly convenient gimmick for avoiding painful choices—or for justifying them. Some European politicians assure us that high unemployment in Europe is due to insufficient competitive strength in relation to the United States and Japan, instead of admitting that Europe is paralyzed by its top-heavy social welfare systems.

The obsession with competitiveness, however, is generating a dangerously aggressive climate. Aside from the absurdity of applying this notion to national economies, constant reference to competitiveness may well lead to world trade confrontations fraught with consequences.

Of course, the leading champions of this belligerent doctrine are opposed to protectionism. They advocate free trade in the hope that their country will win. But what happens in the long run if they turn out to be wrong? Those who overestimate the importance of external factors in "the international economic struggle" will change their position.

In the name of competitiveness, they will declare that we should close national borders to keep other nations from stealing our jobs and high-margin industries. It should be recalled that Mickey Kantor complained during a round of trade negotiations that Japan's trade surpluses were costing America millions of jobs.

GLOBAL COMPETITION

To stay in the race for economic progress, both nations and companies must constantly remain in a state of preparedness. Otherwise, they might become sluggish and get pushed out. Companies are also compelled to anticipate and to adapt, through innovation, investment in research and development, and creation of facilities abroad.

The current competitive context, which pits firms against each other in mortal combat, has also set in motion a dynamic process that has unquestionably contributed to improving living standards throughout the Western world since the end of World War II. The challenge, however, is to maintain this process.

We are now engaged in a very different kind of war.

With economic competition attaining to global status, traditional colonial wars over territory have given way to market conquest and competition for technological mastery.

We are now at economic war on a world scale. Like preceding forms of warfare, today's war has a bearing on government policies and the life styles of people. Although countries now have much less trouble safeguarding their territorial integrity, they must struggle to create jobs and increase national income, sometimes at the expense of other countries. Every country does its utmost to export more goods, services, and intangibles, and to import less.

Heads of state become traveling salesmen
for their economy.

Many heads of state or government have become traveling salesmen who endeavor to promote and favor companies from their country.

They know full well that they will be judged on the basis of the nation's growth rate, since electoral results offer an accurate reflection of what voters think of the government's economic record.

Thus, every politician attempts to highlight his or her contribution to the nation's prosperity in the hope of obtaining a "vote of confidence" on his or her ability to maintain such positive conditions. Not only the business community, but the entire country finds itself locked in a desperate struggle for economic performance and competitive advantage.

Although countries may operate in synergy during periods of buoyant growth–as in the three decades following World War II–their cooperative spirit drops considerably whenever economic slump appears to drag on.

Adjustment requirements have become more acute with the growing complexity of the environment. In the face of new constraints such as lower visibility, greater complexity, and more "unknown quantities" than before, it takes a resolutely optimistic frame of mind to be able to succeed. The trouble in Europe, which suffers from a generally depressed climate, is that people are virtually paralyzed by what they consider to be the irresistible rise of the emerging countries.

THE RISE OF THE EMERGING COUNTRIES

We are currently in a crucial period. For the first time in recent history, the combined gross domestic product of the developing countries will soon be higher than that of the fully developed countries. By the year 2005, the emerging countries will account for 65% of the world market, while the share of wealthy nations will have declined to a mere 35%, as opposed to 60% in 1980.

By 2020, six of the ten leading economies in the world may well be former developing countries.

Three or four of the current G7 countries may no longer have sufficient economic weight to be able to stay in this category (Canada, Great Britain, Italy, and perhaps even France).

Imagine a G10 comprising the ten countries with the largest GNPs in the year 2020. China would be number 1, the United States number 2, Japan number 3, India number 4, Indonesia number 5, Germany number 6, Korea (undoubtedly reunited by then) number 7, Thailand number 8, France number 9, and Taiwan number 10.[1] Even if the order may change, the most striking feature of this ranking is

---

1. World Bank estimates.

the presence of six Asian countries in the future G10, since five of them are not members of today's G7.

The fifteen top countries in 2020 will be the following:
1. China,   2. USA,   3. Japan,   4. India,   5. Indonesia,   6. Germany,
7. Korea,   8. Thailand,   9. France,   10. Taiwan,   11. Brazil,   12. Italy,
13. Russia,   14. Great Britain,   15. Mexico

It should be added that 90% of the world's consumers will be living in the poorer countries. At present, the planet is divided up into several distinct "worlds" (*cf.* the GBN classification in Ch. 1). Whereas, roughly speaking, a scant billion people live in the affluent world, there are nearly four billion people in the developing countries, with over a billion people who have been entirely left out inhabiting the rest of our planet.

> *Is Anglo-Saxon free-market capitalism the only valid model?*

The competitive intelligence of today must be global in scope. It must take into account all countries and all societies in the world, including those whose roots are radically different from those of Western civilization.

Up until the late 1980s, we were living in a bipolar world (the free world and the Communist world) whose two poles roughly correspond to two different forms of "capitalism," one of them based on the free market, and the other one on central state planning.

The disappearance of this binary structure in the 1980s and the trend toward global economic relations have revealed that there are not only two, but several forms of capitalism that are destined to vie with each other.

The question for managers is whether the form of capitalism they are most familiar with can be directly transferred to highly different cultural settings or whether it needs to be adapted.

A company organized along Anglo-Saxon lines will have a hard time adjusting to a technocratic, social welfare-style capitalist structure of the kind found in Germany and Japan, let alone to structures based on family network, of the Chinese variety. The competition of tomorrow will be played out between cultural models (*cf.* Ch. 9).

Up until recently, the Anglo-Saxon model appeared to be the only one truly capable of guaranteeing business success and economic prosperity. Yet we now have to face the facts. The list of the world's hundred leading companies has shifted greatly over the last decade, in terms of both market share and the number of firms from the various areas.

THE ONE HUNDRED LEADING COMPANIES AND THEIR MARKET SHARE, ACCORDING TO CULTURAL AND STRUCTURAL TYPE

Model	Yesterday	Today	Variance
Anglo-Saxon:	66	38	- 28
market share	71%	35%	- 36
European:	25	35	+ 10
market share	23%	27%	+ 4
Japan/Asia:	9	27	+ 18
market share	6%	38%	+ 32
	100	100	

Source: Global Business Network

This table clearly shows that the cards in the world business game are currently being reshuffled among three different forms of capitalism. The Anglo-Saxon "laissez-faire" system is obviously more permeable than the other two forms. The absolute need to pull out of economic recession is creating direct competition between the new markets of the now unified Western Europe, Eastern Europe, and East Asia.

This situation confronts us with a number of new challenges. All our reflexes with regard to manufacturing are typical of highly industrialized countries. Dramatic shifts in the world order thus point the way to major revolutions in the way we think about business.

1. Business activity is becoming global in scope, which implies globalization of competition, with new players to be taken into account.

2. Asset portfolios must be reshuffled.

3. Organizational structures must become global.

These revolutions cannot be forestalled. The way in which we envision the world of today will largely determine our competitive position in the year 2010.

Three Geo-economic Poles, Three Forms of Capitalism

The world's countries are currently clustered together around three geo-economic poles, each one of which has its own philosophy and its own form of capitalism. Let's briefly review them before going on to describe them in greater detail.

Europe

The Enlightenment gave rise to modern European civilization, characterized by values of democracy, freedom, and equality. These values are reflected in respect for human rights and for free-market capitalism, which are considered to provide the guarantee of well-being for all. Should this arrangement fail to meet these requirements, the welfare system transforms the state into a major economic agent that attends to the general interest by focusing on equitable distribution of resources.

Can "humanistic" European capitalism go on redistributing wealth?

The capitalism associated in particular with Germany's Rhineland is based on both the notion of generating wealth through production and engineering, and on redistribution of the wealth produced.

If a social welfare form of capitalism, developing out of the Rhineland or Northern European model, becomes the dominant system in Europe, it will obviously run counter to visions of vast, single-currency markets and of the supremacy of financial institutions, while hindering the short-range profitability of investment.

However, Europe can also reap the benefits of its excellent educational system and training programs, whose high quality runs from elementary school all the way up to elite universities.

Through constant quality improvement, and on the basis of mass consensus, a unified Europe will soon be in a position to create the largest market the continent has ever seen, encouraging strategic thinking at the grass-roots level through workers' codetermination, while developing a resolutely pan-European vision.

In this way, Europe will be able to build large groups dedicated to cooperative partnership in know-how, without necessarily being compelled to create a single, unified social system.

The United States

The formation of the United States reflected a desire to create the ideal European civilization, free of the archaic features of the Old World. Thus, while adopting liberal ideas such as individualism, human rights, democracy, and capitalism, the Americans threw off what they considered the typical shackles of European society, including the following.

• The weight of history, which often stifles enthusiasm, imagination, and progress.

• Hierarchical structures, which distort individual responsibility.

• Socialism and the welfare state, which discourage individual responsibility and weaken a number of virtues inherent in human nature (courage, ambition, and the like).

The Old World and the New World coexist in complementary fashion. American society constitutes a laboratory whose experiments enable Europe to study the future that awaits them. It also serves as a moral conscience in the face of the major political conflicts of the twentieth century (World War I, the rise of totalitarianism, World War II, the break-up of Yugoslavia).

The Americans, in turn, view Europe as a kind of museum, a place in which they can find their roots, since their society was built on European values. Thus, in spite of their obvious differences, the American mentality and the European mentality can be considered close relatives. What does distinguish the United States, however, is its significantly more dynamic character—which works to the disadvantage of European companies.

> *America possesses a "pioneer-style" capitalism*
> *geared to innovation.*

To paraphrase Mark Twain, the announcement that American hegemony is dead has been greatly exaggerated. The capacity of the American people for rapid reaction and adjustment has allowed them to harness their energy toward creative ends.

The logic of a capitalist system concerned solely with catching up is entirely dependent on the existence of an established model, namely the Anglo-Saxon one. Thus, we can reasonably imagine that once the rival economies in Europe and Asia have caught up with the United States (assuming that they do some day), they will reach a sort of saturation point, for lack of another partner capable of providing the needed stimulus.

In contrast, the logic of "pioneer" capitalism, a hallmark of the American mentality, does not bother with established models, but seeks constantly to create and to innovate. The United States is engaged in the industrialization of Latin America, where it enjoys a clear-cut advantage in high technology. For example, the Americans have increased their lead in the fields of telecommunications and computers, which are destined to be the driving forces of economic growth, just as the automobile industry and the highway network were in the post-war period.

Thus, through a strategy based on innovation planned at high level, America can use its political leadership to establish an impregnable position in world competition, by demanding ever higher standards of quality. In addition, it will enjoy unchallenged rule as a result of its control over markets and its exceptional mastery of customer relations.

Asia

Following the Meiji era of modernization in Japan, and especially since the economic miracle that the country experienced after World War II, the West became convinced that its ideas had deeply penetrated Japanese society. After all, people reasoned, the Far Eastern elite was studying business administration, economics, and political science at the leading American and European universities. All the evidence seemed to indicate that Japan, the "dragons", and finally China, with its special economic zones, were on the verge of reproducing America's spectacular success. It turns out, however, that this apparent adoption of Western culture by the Far Eastern countries barely went beyond the technical field.

We are thus witnessing an unprecedented historical phenomenon, i.e. a highly original merging of Western and Eastern culture in the Asia-Pacific region. While Asia has unquestionably embraced capitalism and the market economy, it still refuses to assimilate democratic values, human rights, Western individualism, and the welfare state.

The Asian economies combine the traditional components of capitalism like international financial markets, technological innovation, and the easing of trade restrictions with the principle of social inequality. Mr. Goh Chok Tong, Singapore's prime minister, offered a good summary of this philosophy, saying "We believe that a balance must be struck between the rights of the individual and his obligations toward the community... In some cases, we may restrict these rights in order to safeguard the general interest."

As regards democratic values in particular, there is therefore an enormous gap between the American and European economic poles, on the one hand, and the Asian pole on the other hand. Westerners have such a hard time understanding a world in which a growing number of non-Western powers play an important part that they tend to focus on the economic similarities between regions, while paying scant attention to the tremendous cultural differences that subsist. In Asia, the Western model is used as a mere means to develop the economy, with no concern for human rights or democracy. This unique Asian culture has two basic ingredients.

• The humiliating experience of colonial domination, which remains a source of deep resentment against the West.

• The desire to preserve an authentic cultural identity, while advancing down the road of modernity and economic success.

Partnership and creativity are the chief assets
of Asian network-capitalism.

The question arises whether Japan will still be able to serve as the driving force of the Asian economy, once it has gotten past its current identity crisis, or whether the Chinese diaspora will take over this function. In spite of important differences with regard to the rest of the region, Japan has retained a way of thinking which, although somewhat Westernized, remains fundamentally similar to that of its neighbors.

• To Asians, a company is above all a "living" thing, rather than a mere combination of know-how designed solely to serve the shareholders' interests.

• Asians are always concerned with the long range, both regarding R & D—as in the other models—and finance.

• In Asian capitalism, shareholders do not take priority over the company's workers and managers.

This frame of mind, which might be termed "relationship-oriented," reveals its full significance in the technique developed by the Japanese in the 1980s called "analysis of latent needs." This method connects companies to their customers and suppliers in a long-term alliance aimed at determining latent needs and jointly working out the technical solutions for meeting them. The supplier-producer-customer entity thereby becomes a learning structure.

The existence of such a concept shows that Japanese creativity—unlike American creativity—depends more on planning than on spontaneity, with the considerable advantage of creating the market at the same time as the product.

In such a scenario, strategy is centered on middle management and workers. It thus establishes powerful links of partnership between company members, customers, and suppliers by building joint projects conducive to creative innovation.

The first of these three worlds which we will examine in detail here is certainly the most distant one, i.e. Asia. The reason for this is that in the current context of globalization, its achievements are a source of great fascination—perhaps even too great.

The Arrival on the Scene of Asia as the Start of Globalization

With the end of the cold war, the Western period in international politics draws to a close. From now on, world politics will revolve around the relations between Western and non-Western civilizations, as well as around the relations between the various civilizations composing the non-Western world.

All eyes are now on Asia. Owing to the size of certain markets, chiefly the Chinese market, any new competitor of a leading Western firm that succeeds in making a significant breakthrough on one of these mega-markets could quickly turn into a threatening rival.

> *Asia's project is one of modernization without Westernization.*

Asia is currently attempting to modernize without becoming Westernized in the process. East-Asian capitalism hopes to go beyond the Western model in terms of independence and economic performance through incorporation of various features of the Western economy into its culture, while jealously maintaining the region's traditions. A large number of Asian countries, including China, Burma, Vietnam, and Indonesia, openly advocate such a cultural amalgamation.

It would be a mistake to believe that Asians are becoming more and more like Westerners all the time. Such an assumption is based on mere extrapolation from Europe's past, to such an extent that some people even make dire predictions of civil war and inter-ethnic strife for Asia. The strange thing is that we no longer hear the cannons roar in the Asia-Pacific area, whereas Europe is encircled by an "iron ring" extending from North Africa to the Caucasus. It might therefore be more reasonable to assume that some non-European peoples have reached a stage of development that enables them to move forward, while avoiding the tragic pitfalls of European history.

1. Europe assumes it can secure peace by pursuing a policy aimed at unifying the entire continent and at cutting it off from its periphery, thereby excluding its neighbors from European prosperity. In contrast, the leading East-Asian economies eagerly draw the countries around them (e.g. Vietnam) into their dynamic growth process.

2. Viewing itself as a model for the rest of the world, Europe considers it historically inevitable for all human societies to evolve in the direction of free enterprise, capitalism, and democracy. The trouble with this universalist outlook, however, is that it may lead to an inability to accept the principle of diversity. To put it plainly, the Asia-Pacific region is accustomed to living with diversity, while Europe is not.

3. Europe tries to maintain its relatively high living standards through subsidies and protectionist measures. Asia strengthens itself economically by opening the doors wide to market forces.

Should we be more impressed by the East-Asian "miracle" than we used to be by the ex-Soviet "miracle?"

The meteoric rise of the newly industrialized countries in Asia is a source of fascination. It simultaneously engenders great optimism regarding the new vistas opening up to companies and pessimistic anxiety over the idea that the Asia-Pacific region might outstrip the West on the world stage. If we are interested in learning from the Asian experience, we should take a close look at the way in which the region adopts the technological breakthroughs achieved elsewhere and incorporates them into its culture. At the same time, however, we should resist the tendency to be dazzled by East-Asian success. The region's recent achievements require deeper investigation.

In the past, other economies have demonstrated exceptional vigor.

Western leaders often reacted with a mixture of stunned admiration and deep apprehension at the spectacular growth rates chalked up by several of the Eastern bloc countries.

Indeed, in spite of the relatively small size and poverty of these economies in comparison to the West, their unusually rapid passage from the agricultural to the industrial world, the higher growth rates they regularly achieved in relation to the most advanced countries, and their ability to equal, or even surpass their American and European rivals in certain technological areas appeared at the time to raise doubts as to the ongoing domination of both the Western powers and the ideologies they espoused.

The leaders of the socialist countries did not share our attachment to the free market and to individual political rights. With increasingly overt self-assurance, they proclaimed the superiority of their system. These were societies that operated well under strong, even authoritarian government and agreed to restricting individual freedom for the common good, to submitting economic life to severe discipline, and to sacrificing the short-term well-being of consumers in order to provide for lasting growth.

The Western attitude toward the Soviet threat in the 1960s prefigures the attitude of today's leaders toward the Asia-Pacific region. Stanford University economist Paul Krugman insists, however, that there is little reason to worry. He points out that economic expansion results from the addition of two sources of growth. On the one hand, there are inputs such as job creation, the rising educational level of workers, and the increase in the mass of physical capital (e.g. plant and equipment, roads), and on the other hand, outputs per unit of input. Although gains in the area of output can sometimes be attributed in the short run to improvements in management or economic policy, their fundamental cause is always to be sought in increases in knowledge.

Sustained growth of per capita income can only
be achieved if output per unit of input rises.

As soon as we engage in this kind of accounting, we discover a basic truth regarding the driving forces behind economic growth. A country cannot achieve sustained growth of its per capita income unless output per unit of input rises. A mere rise in the volume of inputs (e.g. investment in capital equipment and infrastructure) that is not accompanied by more efficient use of these inputs suffers sooner or later from the law of diminishing returns. Growth fueled solely by inputs is eventually destined to run out of steam.

This insight sheds new light on the limits encountered by the Soviet economy in the 1960s, while also making it possible to put the recent East-Asian boom into perspective. In the case of the Soviet Union, growth figures above all reflected a rapid rise in inputs. The country's planning authorities had succeeded in mobilizing a colossal volume of resources. Millions of men and women left the countryside and flocked into the factories in the cities, where they put in long, grueling hours of labor. Mass education accomplished a tremendous leap forward. And above all, a steadily rising share of the industrial wealth created was reinvested in the construction of new plant and equipment. Yet all of this was not sufficient to save the Soviet economy from the inevitable slowing down of growth that befalls any economy running essentially on inputs.

Although it would obviously be tricky to venture the same forecast for East Asia, given the considerable differences between this region today and the Soviet Union of 1960, there are nonetheless a number of rather striking similarities. Like the Soviet Union, the newly industrialized countries in Asia owe much of their rapid growth to their astonishing mobilization of resources. The region's expansion over the past several years seems to be fueled by an extraordinary increase in the volume of inputs like capital and labor, rather than by actual gains in efficiency.

Singapore offers a typical example of such a mobilization of resources. From 1966 to 1990, the share of the population participating in the work force jumped from 27% to 51%. During the same period, the educational level of wage and salary earners made impressive strides forward. Whereas in 1966, over half of them had no formal education, in 1990, two thirds of them were graduates of secondary school. But above all, the country made colossal investment efforts in plant and equipment. Investment (financed essentially by the country's savings) went from 11% to over 40% as a share of total output.

It follows that Singapore's dazzling success was mainly due to radical shifts in behavior that cannot be expected to occur ever again. In a single generation, the proportion of the population participating in the work force nearly doubled, and it can hardly double again. A barely literate work force was replaced by a mass of workers who have finished high school, whereas it is highly unlikely that the majority of the next generation of workers will get doctoral degrees. Last of all, a 40% investment level already stretches the imagination, while a 70% level would be downright absurd. We therefore have every reason to assume that Singapore will be unable to maintain the high growth rates achieved in this exceptional period. Although the East Asian economies have experienced a spectacular boom in recent years, this growth rate is clearly not sustainable.

Asian growth is likely to slow down soon.

The likeliest scenario for the East Asian economies is that, far from surpassing us, they will soon drop down to growth rates similar to ours, i.e. lower, and therefore easier to maintain. Thus, instead of fearing Asia, we should consider the present situation an opportunity—and a short-lived one at that—to penetrate these markets and take advantage of their stunningly high growth rates before they settle into a pattern typical of developed countries. A word of caution is in order, however. It would be a serious mistake to confuse energetic action with rash behavior. In order to get a foot in the Asian door, we have to be both well informed and level-headed. Furthermore, the East Asian markets are in any case extremely large, and the larger a market is, the more costly it becomes to enter it once it has matured.

In terms of culture and style of capitalism,
Europe is closer to Japan than to America.

From now on, we are required to adjust to several different forms of capitalism and to the cultural settings that condition them.

Although it may seem paradoxical, the European vision of capitalism, which for historical reasons places considerable emphasis on social and human factors, turns out to be closer to Japanese or Asian conceptions than to the Anglo-American vision. We will return to this point in Chapter 9, describing in detail the responses of leaders from each of these capitalist cultures to current dilemmas (see the Appendix for a summary of a number of the questions and the various response percentages by country). This is perhaps an asset that European companies eager to break into Asian markets might wish to stress (provided, of course, that they make the necessary efforts for bridging the still enormous cultural gap between these two regions of the world).

Some industries (e.g. telecommunications, information technology, transport) are already showing the way. Since they are compelled to achieve world-wide scope and interconnection, and in light of the

significant investments they have to make and their need for networking, they must develop strategic alliances with their competitors if they
want to survive and succeed. This obligatory participation in broader
industry groups greatly helps them to deal with cultural problems that
would otherwise be hard to solve.

> *If European firms want to get a foothold in*
> *Asia, they will have to establish partnerships.*

As François Périgot, head of the French employers' federation, once
put it, "Instead of complaining about how the dynamic Asian economies are conquering our Western markets, our companies should set
out to conquer Asia, since it is a region that for several years has
enjoyed the high growth rates that we're lacking." To stay competitive,
today's firms have to take all the regions in the world into account,
especially East Asia, Eastern Europe, and Latin America.

Several questions arise at this stage, however. To set up shop in
Asia, can we apply methods that were developed in an Anglo-Saxon,
Judeo-Christian context? Are these methods which we know so well
actually suited to a new world of prosperity whose reflexes, ways of
thinking, and culture are clearly miles apart from ours? In other words,
is our liberal, free-market mind-set perceived in the same fashion by
the Chinese, the Koreans, the Japanese, or the Indians? Does the very
idea of capitalism have the same meaning everywhere?

The lack of understanding evinced by the Western business community regarding the nature of Asian tradition may well provoke a
justified defensive reaction on the part Asian businesspeople. They
rightly suspect the West of pursuing a strategy of neocolonial domination. In their eyes, Western firms are attempting to disregard the
elementary rules of political and cultural harmony. The only way to
achieve such harmony between the two cultures involved is to seek out
local partners. Knowing how to establish strategic alliances with local
talent in these regions of the world may well prove to be of vital
importance.

Companies that simply try to break into Asian markets on their own
may find themselves being accused of imperialism. In contrast, by
establishing true dialogue based on an acceptance of difference, we can
achieve fruitful exchange. Owing to the difficult cultural problems to
be solved, the easiest and the most constructive approach may be to
scout around for local allies. When the future is at stake, it is advisable
to live by the following motto: "It is better to share a good deal with
someone than to have a bad deal all to yourself."

Globalization Also Rhymes with Americanization

As the leading players in the process of globalization that has by now spread to most of our planet, the Americans apply to the world economy the Messianic fervor which used to be limited to their political system and their general world view. The United States can pride itself on economic results that are the envy of its major partners in Japan and particularly in Europe, which appears extremely fragile at present. This makes it the uncontested world leader, both in real terms and at the World Economic Forum held each year at Davos, in Switzerland.

> *The buoyancy of the American economy lends weight to the Messianic message conveyed by the Anglo-Saxon system.*

Thus, the United States clearly played the leading role at the 1997 forum, devoted to "building a network society." Present in full force at this small Swiss resort town, the country's political leaders showed great self-assurance, its corporate leaders a sense of superiority, and its economists more than a touch of arrogance.

To Joseph Stiglitz, President Clinton's chief economist, who was on his way to a new position at the World Bank, the U.S. economy was in "an ideal situation, the best it's ever known over the past thirty years." His political opponents such as the economist Michael Boskin, George Bush's former chief advisor, made no effort to contradict him. Since the forum, stock market prices have continued to skyrocket, a trend which, according to Alan Greenspan, head of the Federal Reserve Board, by no means reflects some "irrational exuberance" of the market, but rather "rational exuberance," as Mr. Stiglitz claimed. Growth remains strong, regular, and free of inflation. Productivity is rising faster and faster. The nation's companies boast of higher profits than ever before. Countless jobs have been created. In a word, it's the American dream come true.

If we are to believe the economists, this dream is not about to turn into a nightmare. They are virtually unanimous in predicting that job creation and profitability will continue along on their upward curve well beyond 1997. As they see it, America has entered a profoundly new era, the era of the "new economics."

> *The alternative economic "top models" have not stood the test of time as well.*

In contrast, the Europeans—and even the Japanese to a certain extent—appear to this triumphant America to be hopelessly bogged down in old economics and consequently to suffer from anaemic growth, mass unemployment, and ailing companies. The example that is eagerly put forward is that of the automobile industry. Although it was assumed for years, in a sort of diabolical vision, that the Japanese would win the battle, it turned out that the Americans inflicted a crushing defeat on them.

The criticisms leveled in the past at Anglo-Saxon capitalism are now contemptuously dismissed. Lawrence Summers, number two at the U.S. Treasury, states that just a few years ago, it was rather fashionable to predict the decline of America. The country was going to fall apart because it never adopted a real industrial policy, because it succumbed to the sirens of high finance and speculation. The Europeans and the Japanese had no trouble scoffing at the "short-termism" plaguing America. Today, in fact, it seems quite clear that America is not only in excellent shape, but has also recovered its imperial supremacy in all new technologies, owing to companies that, as it turns out, have much more of a long-range perspective than was thought.

In the early 1980s, everyone raved on about the "German model." Then, about five years ago, the "Japanese model" was in the limelight. Both of them are now in crisis. In economics as well as in fashion, the top model career offers precious little security.

The doubts frequently expressed in the United States as to Europe's ability to meet the challenges inherent in the global economy usually focus on the excessive generosity of the welfare state, held responsible for lack of competitive strength, and on what is interpreted as the Old World's hostility toward entrepreneurs. Unlike the United States, some American economists contend, which has added 45 million new jobs, Europe has failed to create a single job since 1970. As for Japan, rigid structures and excessive bureaucracy have, they claim, held back the economy of a country that may not really belong to Asia.

Europe has little credibility when it puts forward an alternative model, owing to its double-digit unemployment rates and the extent to which it now lags behind in the fields of technological and financial innovation.

The American Model: a Dead-End for Europe?

It is hard to say whether Europe and even Asia can escape the "American model" or whether globalization amounts to little more than the "Americanization" of the world.

On the one hand, John Sweeny, the president of the AFL-CIO, who was present at the 1997 Davos forum along with other union leaders, warned that considering America a model would "lead Europe down a dead-end," since such a system cannot be applied to radically different social contexts. Countries like Russia that have tried to import the American neoliberal model have mostly met with failure. In any assessment of the U.S. economy, it should be borne in mind that between 1979 and 1995, large-scale downsizing in the United States destroyed

45 million jobs, that two thirds of all laid-off workers had to accept jobs at lower wages than before, and that one quarter of all American children start off their lives below the poverty level. "Inequality has reached its highest level since the Great Depression," concluded Sweeny.

On the other hand, the CEOs of General Electric, Nestlé's, and various other multinational corporations retorted that the transfer of the American model to Europe was simply "inevitable."

The mainstream opinion is more balanced, however. Most observers merely contend that the American model is not entirely exportable, that it undoubtedly needs to be adapted to different national settings, that Margaret Thatcher proved to be a bold, but too dogmatic disciple. As for the Americans themselves, although they indulge in the luxury of deploring the inequality engendered or sustained by their model, they nonetheless end up judging their system the way Churchill once spoke of democracy, i.e. "It is the worst system there is, except for all the others."

So is America really a model? No, but it may be a source of inspiration. Many Europeans would certainly agree with Louis Schweitzer, the CEO of Renault, that we have to examine the American model in order to determine what is worth keeping. The ability of the United States to produce the likes of Bill Gates, the efficiency of its companies, and the flexibility of its labor market are endlessly stressed.

However, another point must be added to all these arguments for and against the American model. "When it comes to applying the American model, the Americans know how to do it a thousand times better than anyone else."

The model is hard to copy.

For a number of reasons, in fact, copying this model might be rather risky business.

• The United States represents a vast, unified, open market with 250 million inhabitants that speak the same language, with a large middle class, on a continent unusually rich in natural resources.

• The currency used on this market plays a global role, if for no other reason than that the chief energy source is booked in dollars.

• The country's skilled, educated work force (25% of all workers have been to college) is renewed each generation by new immigrants.

With their booming economy and their undisputed monopoly over the industries of the future, the Americans show the natural, unselfconscious arrogance of a country that knows it is dominant. Yet this does not prevent them from recognizing the drawbacks that come with such advantages. Lawrence Summers has singled out three significant imperfections in the American model.

1) The low level of savings.

2) The failure of the system to integrate Black youth. The mortality rate among young African-Americans is higher than the mortality rate of children in Asia. A young Black is more likely to wind up in prison than to land a steady job.

3) The decline in civic spirit. There is no longer any attachment to the national community. A great deal has changed since the time when Kennedy proclaimed, "Ask not what your country can do for you, but what you can do for your country."

Thus, before we import such a model, we must analyze it, and perhaps take inspiration from it. But adopting it uncritically would be a disaster.

RADICAL SHIFTS IN THE ENVIRONMENT

3

In this era of radical change, it is exceedingly difficult to identify the major trends, to single out the key elements that foreshadow upcoming breaks, and to gauge the impact these elements will have on the competitive world in which companies operate. Our extremely complex environment is made up of a large number of cross-currents, which engender counter-currents, which in turn contain other, divergent currents. To put it plainly, there no longer is any single response, but a multitude of possibilities—and opportunities.

Without claiming to be exhaustive, we will attempt to describe four basic trends at work in the current period of transition: the phenomenon of globalization, the restructuring of national economies, incessant technological change, and the information and knowledge society.

The New Economic Challenges

The globalization of our economies, as we know, entails rapid movement of capital, information circulating in record time, intensified competition, a growing number of products that ignore all borders, and the interconnection of financial markets. All of this has sparked a debate on the global versus the local, to which we will return in Chapter 9. For the time being, a few brief remarks should suffice.

• **The evolution of economic structures.** Public services are losing ground to privatizations, while large corporations increasingly give way to a vast constellation of small firms. To incorporate the latest technologies, our economies have entered a process of basic restructuring that engenders a climate of suffering, with unemployment rising to alarming levels.

• **The shifting nature of work.** Virtual companies, outsourcing, and telecommuting are all developing rapidly. In the United States, Japan, and Great Britain, the ranks of the self-employed have swollen. The state of the work force has changed dramatically as a result of the growing number of working women, the increase in part-time and temporary work (+ 60% in 1995), and the emergence of new forms of activity, all of which has an obvious effect on consumption patterns.

EXAMPLE

■ IN THE EARLY YEARS OF THE DEPARTMENT STORES, in the late nineteenth century, the wide variety of goods offered, the high social status associated with shopping there, and easy access to downtown areas brought such stores handsome profit margins. In addition, suppliers felt extremely flattered to have their products displayed in department stores.

Gradually, however, competition in distinct categories emerged. First came heavy household appliances, then hi-fi equipment, followed by apparel (e.g. Benetton), and more recently by toys (Toys'R Us).

The managers of the traditional department stores responded by emphasizing "commodity" products and upscale products with little practical use. The need to cut costs, however, has led to a decline in product and service quality. Finding themselves on the defensive, the department stores wind up doing little more than "managing the past."

In the United States, for example, K-Mart and above all Walmart (as well as chains like The Limited and The Gap) have succeeded in taking over what used to be the "bread and butter" of Bloomingdale's, Saks Fifth Avenue, Macy's, and ultimately even Sears, while putting these stores in a precarious position. Nor is this problem limited to America. Although Asia has for the most part managed to escape this trend (since the classical department store style is still alive and well there), British, Australian, Scandinavian, and French department stores are currently faced with much the same difficulties as their American counterparts.

The problem confronting them is not a financial one. It is a much more serious problem, one of a sociological nature that results from shifts in consumer life styles. Traffic congestion in downtown areas; urban stress; the steadily rising number of working women, who therefore have less time for shopping; the irresistible rise of mega-shopping malls in the suburbs that have a clearcut advantage in terms of price and location; and the declining concern for the social status traditionally derived from shopping at the "right" place all suggest that the sociological changes associated with postmodernity are unfavorable to traditional distribution channels.

Global Strategic Trends

Some of the basic trends at work affect all areas of corporate capabilities. The previous chapter discussed the long neglected economic boom in East Asia and the "superstar syndrome" resulting from heightened competition on a world scale. In this passage, we will briefly deal with ecological problems, the aging of the population and demographic explosion, and the radical shifts occuring in the nature of work.

An Aging Population in the West, Population Explosion Elsewhere

Two billion new workers from the developing countries can handle most production activities and a growing number of service activities at infinitely lower cost than can their counterparts in developed countries, who used to accomplish most of such work. This context has a strong influence on many companies, particularly since the work force in the industrial countries is rapidly aging.

• *The aging of the population in the wealthy countries.* This phenomenon should lead us to pay closer attention to the rest of the world, which is in the throes of a demographic explosion. Whereas the average age in the developing countries is 20, it is 40 in the developed countries. This suggests the importance of creating new goods and services on our Western markets in order to meet the needs of consumers. The elderly do not, however, constitute an actual market, but merely a new market segment.

• *Bloated cities.* At the dawn of the twentieth century, cities represented 10% of world population. By the year 2020, it is estimated that the urban population will have reached 60% of the total, in spite of a decline in the average rate of population growth.

The Rising Concern for Health and the Environment

The quality of life has become a major concern in our society. Increasing attention is paid to rising health care costs, the development of alternative ways of healing, the danger of global warming, pollution and insidious threats to the food chain (e.g. Chernobyl, mad cow disease).

Holistic conceptions of health are creating a
formidable potential for new products.

With the growing trend away from Cartesian dualism, which radically separates mind from body, our society is increasingly turning
toward a homogeneous vision of health that encompasses both mind
and body. This explains why we are spending more and more money
on alternative medicine and on a wide array of techniques designed to
help "the mind feel good in the body." This tendency holds tremendous potential in terms of new markets and new kinds of products.

EXAMPLE

■ IN GERMANY, CONSUMER CHOICE OF PRODUCTS is guided largely
by the ability of companies to come up with original, spectacular
responses to the problem of recycling and to build concern for
environmental protection into the product itself. Any company
offering products in Germany without at the same time providing
detailed responses to ecological questions would immediately be
disqualified.

Companies must become a driving force behind
efforts at environmental protection, instead of
merely submitting to them.

All the contemporary questions related to the environment–air pollution, the use of the earth, biotechnology–are concerns that should be
incorporated into a wide range of thinking on sales and competition.
The point is not merely to win over worried consumers, but also to take
seriously developments that in the long run constitute real threats to
industrial activity.

At the same time that such concerns have come to the fore, global
companies increasingly appear to be the main culprits in the area of
environmental disorder. Whereas in the 1960s, governments were
accused of polluting the environment, it is the multinationals that are
now being targeted.

This shift in public opinion has gone hand in hand with the diminishing role of the state in the economy. At present, the largest corporations in the world have comparable economic weight to existing
nation-states. The five leading companies in terms of sales (GM, Ford,
Toyota, Exxon, and Royal Dutch Shell) accounted for 4% of world GDP
in 1995.

As a result, companies cannot escape a certain ethical responsibility
in relation to the well-being of people, their standard of living, and
their values. Although often eluded, these issues will soon widen the

gap between the companies capable of responding adequately and all the others.

A LONG LIST OF DANGERS

• The hole in the ozone layer may increase air pollution in urban areas. As a result of the acid vapors and toxic particles it contains, the air adversely affects visibility.

• Due to the increasing number of cars in the world, pollution from automobiles has recently reached alarming proportions in large cities, with higher and higher carbon dioxyde levels being recorded.

• In less than twenty years' time, we have witnessed a dramatic increase in the number of floods causing loss of human life. From 1930 to 1989, such flooding has increased by a factor of over 100. As regards weather disasters of all kinds, the increase has been by a factor of 360. Between 1930 and 1989, the number of typhoons has increased tenfold.

• Underground water seeping into our water supplies may do considerable harm to the industries of water purification and distribution.

• Climatic shifts may adversely affect whole industry segments. And the possible consequences of global warming give even greater cause for concern. At a recent conference in Brussels on the question, it was said that 4° more might be enough to melt down a large part of the ice caps in Greenland and the Antarctic, which could raise the level of the oceans by as much as 80 feet.

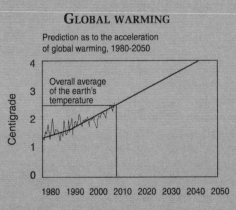

GLOBAL WARMING

Prediction as to the acceleration
of global warming, 1980-2050

Centigrade

Overall average
of the earth's
temperature

1980 1990 2000 2010 2020 2030 2040 2050

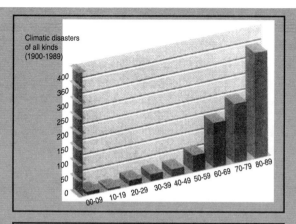

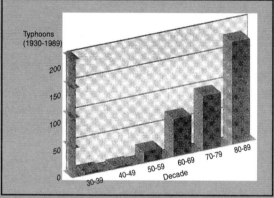

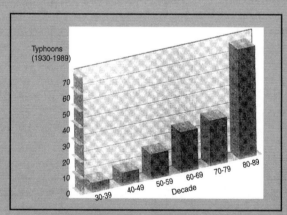

The number of climatic disasters registered up until 1989 that have caused over 20 deaths has risen exponentially in the twentieth century. (Source: USAID/OFDA).

Major Social Changes

Let's take a brief look at five social changes that appear to be decisive.

- **The reshaping of family life and the role of the individual in society.** Single-parent households constitute a new social nexus, family ties are breaking down, and individuality becomes paramount. This can even be seen in the layout of contemporary houses and apartments (kitchens and bathrooms are getting larger, while dining rooms are on the way out). Such changes also affect the way in which society is structured. For example, the middle class appears to be on the decline.

- **The weakening or even severing of social ties, as seen in rising violence.** A key indicator of this trend is the growing number of prisoners in most developed countries. In 1940, school systems were chiefly confronted with problems such as students breaking the rules, talking in class without permission, chewing gum, and refusing to walk in line. Today, the schools have to deal with heavy drinking, drug abuse, teenage pregnancy, and violence that sometimes goes as far as homicide. The psychological profile of school children has undergone considerable change.

- **The decay of social institutions.** In this context of rapidly accelerating upheaval, faith in institutions like government, churches, and even the family has dropped to an all-time low. As a result, the desire to give new meaning to work and other activities will probably be one of the essential factors for understanding the world of the future. Many people today, especially young people, no longer view their jobs as the only area in which to realize themselves. They seek to achieve a more satisfying balance between the various aspects of their lives.

- **High unemployment (in much of Europe).** The developed countries produce an abundance of material things that stands in bold contrast to newly emerging forms of shortage, particularly as regards available jobs. A good many otherwise wealthy countries are now plagued with alarming levels of structural unemployment that raise the likelihood for any one person to fall victim to crime.

- **Mosaic society.** We must now prepare to live in a multicultural, multilingual environment. Cultural diversity has brought about the fragmentation of values, tastes, and life styles, not to mention the rising incidence of mixed marriage. Thus, the highly "inbred" nature of Japanese society does not really work to the country's advantage, since it discourages adjustment to or exchange with other cultures. The global-local dilemma takes on new significance, as the trend toward globalization is accompanied by the assertion of local particularities that have to be reckoned with (*cf.* Ch. 9).

Today's Sales Revolutions

Let's now consider both the inextricable bond between product and service, which currently involves the weakening of traditional distribution channels, and the impact of marketing on social trends such as the development of telecommuting, high consumption among the elderly, the growing gap between rich and poor, and rising awareness of social problems.

The Shifting Notion of Service and of Distribution Channels

• **The (crazy) marriage between product and service.** These two functions are by now so closely intertwined that it wouldn't be too far-fetched to speak of a "provice-serduct" couple. More and more consumers are demanding custom service tailored to their life styles, schedules, and preferences. No company today can afford to ignore this essential asset: consumers' insistence on the quality of the service linked to the product they buy.

EXAMPLE

■ ONCE THE NUMBER OF COMPETING TV CHANNELS reaches the hundred mark, consumers have to seek the assistance of an intermediary who is both informed of their tastes and needs, and capable of establishing a personalized grid of priorities. Consumers will be increasingly willing to pay a high price, not so much for the product itself (i.e. special interest channels) as for this kind of facilitating service.

• **The disintegration of conventional distribution channels, or "disintermediation."** The rise in custom service goes hand in hand with the trend toward bypassing middlemen. With the possibility of connecting up anywhere at any time, consumers can deal directly with producers whenever distributors fail to meet their needs. The quantum leap represented by information technology allows for deeper knowledge of products and therefore requires a better "fit" between promise and delivery.

EXAMPLE

■ THE SUCCESS OF WAREHOUSE SALES in the United States (e.g. by chains like Costco) clearly demonstrates how far disintermediation has already gone. The same can be said of electronic shopping on Internet.

New Consumer Behavior Patterns

Owing to the rise in telecommuting, companies will increasingly be forced to reach consumers at home. Our traditional mind-set leads us to imagine our customers working five days a week at steady jobs in fixed locations, with clearly defined hierarchical relations and fringe benefits. In fact, however, a growing percentage of the population now works at virtual, non-stable jobs. The behavior of such consumers will no longer fit in with traditional patterns.

New consumers call for new messages.

Companies must convey new messages to its customers for the following reasons.

• There is a growing awareness of social and environmental problems.

• As a result of the aging of the population, elderly consumers have taken on increasing importance (*cf.* the graph below).

• The widening gap between rich and poor is leading to new power relations and new buying patterns.

Aging of the Population in the Developed Countries

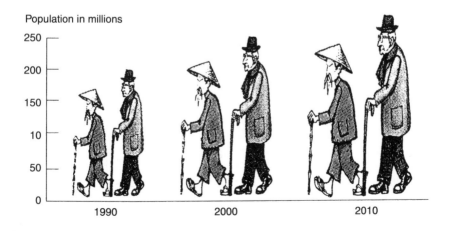

Population in millions

Baby Boom in the Developing Countries

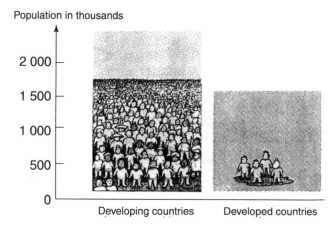

Population in thousands

Developing countries   Developed countries

Technological Change

In the 1970s, the Club of Rome envisioned a future situation of economic stagnation as a result of anticipated depletion of energy sources and raw material supplies. This scenario has since been belied by the development of alternative energy sources and composite materials. The trend is now continuing, owing to new information technology and biotechnology.

Of course, major technological breakthroughs are always followed by periods of relative calm. But ours is an epoch marked by much greater change than in any previous historical period. Revolutionary technologies that reinforce each other are producing a radical upheaval in such fields as new materials, genetics, biotechnology, information science, and space technology.

Owing to their exceptional scope, recent technological innovations no longer have an evolutionary, but rather a revolutionary character (e.g. memory chip cards or transgenic food). These rapid, powerful, incessant revolutionary waves are profoundly changing the way in which we work.

The long periods of stability that have always come after breakthroughs, during which no major changes in industrial production, consumption, or infrastructure occurred, are getting shorter all the time – even fading out entirely in recent years. This new curve of technological evolution marks a decisive component in our strategic outlook, a fundamental turning point in the logic of progress, as change no longer seems to "settle down" the way it used to. We appear to be living in an era of "perpetual transition."

We will now offer a quick review of tomorrow's key technologies.

Genetics

It is in the field of life science technology that the breakthroughs are arguably the most spectacular. Recent cloning experiments carried out in Scotland on the famous Dolly and Polly sheep point the way to the production, in the milk of livestock, of medication that previously had to be synthesized in laboratories.

And since it is possible to extract DNA in one place and recombine it elsewhere, we can also imagine grafting a firefly's DNA on a bee, thus equipping it with a sort of electric lamp that would enable it to gather honey during the night.

However, such technological wonders may soon meet with stiff resistence. Cloning has rekindled all kinds of age-old fears and fantasies. Although humanity has been engaged in genetic manipulation for centuries in the animal and vegetable kingdoms, people today now imagine human clones that call to mind sinister memories of a not-too-distant past.

One can't help wondering whether job applicants in the future will be required to present not only their resumés, but also their genetic maps. If the famous Soviet skater, who just died at the age of 28, had known his genetic map, he might have envisioned other life scenarios for himself.

Neurosciences

The twenty-first century will witness the flowering of the neurosciences. Our basic conceptions may well be revolutionized as a result. We are on the verge of discovering how the mind works. To mention only one example, Prozac has undoubtedly already brought about a revolution in the treatment of depression.

New Materials

Up until now, we have been living in a world in which everything was created and found in nature. The use of stone, iron, and wood all meant that we were limited by the inherent characteristics of the materials. In the future, we will certainly be able to modify whatever nano-characteristics we like. There will be practically no limits to what we can do.

We have entered the realm of inorganic chemistry, and we will be experiencing an invisible revolution that will radically change the nature of materials. It will soon be possible to stuff the walls with microprocessors. For example, ceramics are already being used in processes of inorganic chemistry to replace materials of all sorts. The R & D departments in many high-tech companies are now working on ways to modify materials to give them the specifications they desire.

Patent registrations to control new materials are on the increase, in the fields of biotechnology, molecular modelling, and nano-technologies on DNA. Tomorrow, our systems will process matter the way computers process data today, running down the list of quality features: speed, reliability, flexibility, zero defect, computer-aided production, and cloning. Warfare has already moved far along this path.

During the Gulf War, technological advances enabled the allied forces to hit their targets with hitherto unimaginable accuracy.

Nano-Technology

In addition to making machines, we now know how to make machines that make machines as well. We are thus familiar with machines large and small. The interesting question is just how far miniaturization can actually go.

New Information Technology

Computing power doubles every few months, according to Moore's famous law. Every six months, the capacity of computers goes up. Every eighteen months, the cost of information capacity drops 30%, while microchip performance doubles. Computer equipment is now 8,000 times cheaper than it was thirty years ago. If the automobile industry had developed at a similar rate, a car would now cost $2 and would travel at the speed of light!

By 2020, factories will be equipped with an incalculable number of robots capable of replacing many traditional physical operations. In 1990, manufacturing companies were already investing more heavily in computer equipment and communications than in all the traditional budget items such as plant and machine tools. Computer-related investment has gone from about 5% to over 40% today.

New information technology is having a decisive impact on business, as the following passage makes clear.

What would happen if all the microprocessors on which computers and other automatic systems run suddenly broke down? The entire economy would grind to a halt almost immediately, or in any case, much faster than with the most paralyzing event we know, namely a nation-wide trucking strike. There would be no more telephone, no more bank transactions, no more electricity, no more mail sorting, no more social security transfer payments. Rail, road, and air transport would be totally disorganized. In the private sphere, the countless household appliances equipped with microchips would stop working. The list could go on indefinitely.[1]

---

1. Gérard Blanc, *Le travail au XXIe siècle* (Dunod, 1995).

The growing computerization of the economy facilitates the transfer of cognitive processes and, in fact, the shift from "experience" industries to "knowledge" industries. The optical fiber network that many countries aim to set up should mark a veritable revolution in management systems. Bill Clinton and Al Gore, who have grasped how vital a change this is, hope to connect all of the United States, then other countries, to this network, and are encouraging investors to contribute heavily to the effort. The result would be a system for circulating information that could make a lasting imprint on life styles.

With the cost per instruction per second now 10,000 times lower than if was twenty years ago, the trajectory followed by data has changed considerably. We have moved from routine messages to multimedia, from essentially in-house information transmission to transmission right to the client or to Internet–a revolutionary arrangement that basically boils down to one big network of interconnected computers.

INTERNATIONAL RATINGS IN NETWORKING

	Phone lines	Mobile phones*	TV sets*	PCs*	Internet servers*
1. United States	602	149	790	350	22
2. Finland	551	262	502	230	43
3. Norway	554	261	425	250	22
4. Denmark	604	241	550	220	10
5. Sweden	683	265	480	170	19
6. Canada	575	114	650	250	17
7. Switzerland	597	78	410	290	13
8. Australia	496	217	482	270	17
9. Iceland	557	157	318	NC	33
10. The Netherlands	509	54	480	170	13
11. New Zeland	470	118	510	200	15
12. Luxemburg	554	97	340	150	5
13. Germany	483	61	550	140	6
14. United Kingdom	489	106	450	120	8
15. Belgium	449	35	486	180	3
16. Japan	480	101	641	150	2
17. Austria	465	62	480	160	7
18. Singapore	473	115	380		8
19. Hong Kong	540	170	359		4
20. France	547	34	580		2

* Per thousand inhabitants.

We are heading towards a knowledge economy.

The development of information technology is leading to the emergence of knowledge society. Data transmission already integrates sound and image at incredible speed, using hypertext and mobile communication systems. The fundamental dividing line will increasingly be between those that have information and those that don't.

Companies operating in an environment conducive to adoption of the new technology hold an undeniable competitive advantage. They can head toward a situation of more variety and less inventory, higher reactivity and lower costs–internally–and thus–externally–greater customer satisfaction and customization. Whoever makes the right moves will get there first–in all these areas.

INFORMATION SHARING

4

The driving force in the transition toward the "new era" (which some refer to as the "knowledge economy") is above all information: digestible, and therefore useful information refracted through the prism of human life, rather than raw, unprocessed information that represents little more than deafening "noise" and paralysis, since it hasn't been decoded.

Because this driving force is clearly one of the most vital for companies to take into account, we have decided to devote an entire chapter to the following two subjects.

• The exponential growth of information marks a revolution comparable in scope to the introduction of the printing press, and thereby ushers in a new era. Information is destined to become the essential resource, the capital commodity of the coming century.

• Information is shared rather than exchanged. Attempts at preventing it from flowing freely not only block the advent of a new society; they also impoverish the information itself, condemning it–and those that hoard it–to rapid obsolescence.

The Times, They Are A'Changin'–and Fast!

The various world civilizations took form with the agricultural era, which was centered on land and the implements needed to work it. They later moved on to the industrial era, whose founding components were the loom and then the steam engine.

Transitions from one major epoch to another in the course of human history (from the paleolithic to the neolithic age, from pastoral and farming life to urban civilization) usually occurred in a gradual, incremental fashion, so much so that people were not always aware of what was happening.

At present, however, we are living in a period of accelerated change, characterized by increasingly frequent quantum leaps in technology–of which we are fully cognizant.

EXAMPLE

■ **WHY IS THERE SUCH PALPABLE TENSION IN CHINA** today? Because the country's various regions are living in different ages. Over half the Chinese population is still directly employed in agriculture, while globalization is rapidly dragging the special economic zones into the age of information.

In contrast, the United States dealt with these upheavals successively rather than simultaneously. In 1900, 80% of the work force was engaged in farming, as opposed to 3% today. In 1950, 65% of the working population was involved in industrial production, a figure that has since dropped to a mere 15%.[1] The U.S. Department of Labor estimates that by the year 2000, nearly half the population will be working in jobs related to information, including data input, processing, retrieval, and analysis. Thus, although the American economy still relies heavily on agriculture and industry, it no longer makes much sense to describe the United States as an industrial nation, let alone a farming country.

Technological progress in the field of communications has deeply affected the various functions inside companies. Between 1989 and 1995, the number of secretaries in the United States declined by 550,000 as a result of the changing nature of their activity. Efficiency gains in traditional industries have combined with relative saturation of the need for heavy equipment to create vast potential opportunity in the service sector and large numbers of available workers.

---

1. James L. Morrison, "Future Scan 2000" (talk given in Washington in July 1996).

■ **AT&T, IBM,** AND **XEROX** have used the productivity gains they made in industrial production to branch increasingly out into service activities.

A FEW FIGURES ON INFORMATION CAPACITY AND TRANSMISSION, TODAY AND TOMORROW

There were 50,000 computers in 1970. There are 150 million computers today, and there should be some 500 million of them by the year 2000.

The processing capacity of every computer has increased several thousandfold, with today's average PC possessing greater capacity than a complex system of ten years ago.

250 million computers are connected to Internet today, a figure that should reach 500 million by the year 2000.

The ranks of the internauts (both households and firms) should swell from 80 million today to 400 million in the year 2000.

The number of web sites, which was 525,000 as of early 1997, should reach the one million mark in the year 2000.

The number of intranet sites (i.e. internal to companies) should rise from 200,000 today to 300,000 by the year 2000. 60% of the world's top 500 companies already possess an intranet system, a figure that should go up to 94% in the year 2000.

On the average, the power of microprocessors doubles every eighteen months, with no deceleration in sight. The already dizzying processing speed, which can be counted in hundreds of millions of operations per second, will increase several thousandfold over the next twenty years.

The capacity of telecommunication lines has been increasing at a comparable rate. In 1977, one copper wire system could handle 12 phone lines. In 1997, two optical fibers could carry up to 70 million lines.

In 1984, it was predicted that the mobile phone market in the United States would reach the 900,000 mark in the year 2000. In 1997, this figure was revised upward–to 40 million phones, generating sales of $60 million a year.

However much these figures have been repeated, they still retain great significance. They bear witness to the deep-going transformation of the economy in the course of only one century.

Internet, or information for everyone at almost
no cost.

By the first years of the twenty-first century, hardware and software will have gotten so sophisticated that if we wish to, we will be able to work without ever leaving home. Wherever your office may be, information technology will enable you to manage totally fragmented structures. This technology will change our lives as radically as television once did. Communication will no longer be a mere possibility; it will become a true extension of our personalities. Mobile phones already give us a fairly good idea of what it means to be connected.

EXAMPLE

■ **AT THE INSEAD** (European Institute for Business Administration) in Fontainebleau, France, where all the students are connected to Internet, the teaching staff has by no means lost its former importance. What actually has occurred is a radical shift in the relationship between student and teacher.

Alvin Toffler coined the term "future shock" to describe accelerated change. The interesting question remains just what meaning should be ascribed to the current innovation spiral.

Today's innovations have one thing in common: they make it possible to accomplish things that humanity already could do, except that they do them faster, with greater power, thereby making systems more dynamic and allowing free energy to be added.

In the nineteenth century, humanity invented or harnessed forces that were superior to its own muscular capacity. In the twentieth century, innovation revolves more around extensions to our sensory organs (telephone, television, telescope).

All complex systems follow the same evolution and reproduction cycle. In order to evolve, a system must enter into an interchange with its environment. It reproduces itself–or facilitates the creation of a new system–by producing an enzyme. We are thus dealing with a process in which one system catalyzes another.

This notion may then be extended to information technology, which is not, in and of itself, the cause of globalization, but merely something that facilitates it. We were the TV generation; our children are the micro-computer generation. The new technology flooding into our companies needs to be brought under control and put to appropriate use.

Artificial intelligence, along with neuronal microchips, should be of invaluable assistance to us.

The first generations of decision-assisting tools already exist, and will increasingly become an integral part of tomorrow's office. The basis for these tools are neuronal networks–a new kind of computer essentially designed for problem solving. Its intelligence comes from neuronal microchips that operate on the same principle as the neurons and synapses inside the human brain.

These neuronal networks will help us surmount a number of crucial barriers that, for the time being, are still blocking the way. For example, voice or text recognition on such networks will be so flexible that it will be able to take on many different forms and be made accessible to large numbers of users. As soon as computers, robots, and other related technologies are hooked up together, the resulting systems might well be capable of running part of our business in our stead, thereby freeing up time for us to innovate, to come up with new ideas and concepts.

Although it is hard to pinpoint exactly how long it will take for these developments to start influencing the way we work, specialists have predicted a number of key dates.

• Voice recognition and handwriting recognition, including understanding of context (c. 2005).

• Automatic translation, involving voice and text recognition in foreign languages (c. 2010).

• The fusion of robotics with neuronal networks in computers capable of understanding and learning (perhaps around 2015 or 2020).

Tomorrow's assistants will become "orchestra conductors" directing technologies that will be taking charge of office work.

The work place will undergo serious changes. All too often, the size and location of the spaces in which people work today are designed on the basis of status, rather than productivity. Offices should change significantly. Smaller, less luxurious, they might serve mainly as meeting places with people from outside the company, or with other partners affiliated to the company's network.

Although the mobile office is technically workable, there is still considerable reluctance about it.

The full-time, salaried job in a fixed location, which was a hallmark of industrial society, is inevitably giving way to part-time jobs or work at home. Many former wage and salary earners will have no other option than to become self-employed, to develop their own projects, or to accept several time-share jobs, a choice that some people have already made for family reasons or because they see it as a way to improve the quality of their lives.

If we concentrate narrowly on a single kind of job (with compensation being dispensed on the employer's premises) that no longer corresponds to the requirements of today, we run the risk of mistaking what will be the rule tomorrow for a mere stopgap measure. In the not-too-distant future, full-time workers with steady jobs will be in the minority. They will form the hard core of a company's skill pool, around which a large constellation of temporary workers, sub-contractors, self-employed people and other members of the company's external networks will gravitate.

The new possibilities offered by teleconferencing and telecommuting will some day do away with the need to bring together the various participants in a project at a single physical location. Companies will thus be able to reduce both their work force and maintenance costs on office space. The crucial point in developing work outside the office will be for company executives around the world to demonstrate that they can function just as effectively using e-mail, voice mail, and video-conferencing on a large scale.

There still remains, however, a major psychological barrier to tele-commuting, which is that when all has been said and done, people like to congregate. Belonging to a clan often takes on greater importance even than protecting your turf. Job-related socializing and camaraderie become essential.

Work at home is therefore unlikely to develop as quickly as we might like, but it nonetheless holds out considerable hope for achieving a harmonious balance between work and the quality of life. It is no longer a utopian dream to anticipate that today's metropolitan areas might become decongested and that abandoned rural areas might come back to life. All it takes is a little bit of imagination.

The Age of Technology Galore

Today's information technology will play a predominant role in the future. We have to accept the obligation to invest carefully in both the necessary equipment and training in how to use it. Instead of confining the new information technology to this or that department, we should put it in the very center of the strategic process.

With the help of this technology, we will be in a position to reengineer our activities. More than ever before, we have to imagine and invent new ways of exploiting technical advances to enhance our managerial and operational capabilities.

The new white-collar "knowledge workers" who are able to stay abreast of developments will become the middle management of tomorrow.

Tomorrow's economy will be dominated by
"soft" factors.

"Soft" is rapidly pushing out "hard" in today's business world. Microsoft's market value is now greater than that of General Motors, although GM still has much higher sales figures.

Digitalization and virtual reality will constitute the world of our children, thereby modifying the way in which they learn. The spectacular development of this world will lead them toward a different relationship to images.

In the years to come, we will be seeing new combinations of functional technologies made possible by the incorporation of microprocessors into countless tools used in daily life, which will become easier and more enjoyable as a result.

EXAMPLE

■ **AT HOME, CURRENTLY EXISTING INFORMATION TECHNOLOGY** will enable us to fit out an adjoining area to the bathroom with instruments providing relevant data on blood pressure, heart beat, stress, and the like. If you are on the anxious, paranoid side, you can even arrange to be hooked up while you're sleeping to a device that gives you the vital indicators as soon as you wake up. This is by no means a science-fiction scenario. In the near future, every home can be equipped with its own, electronically wired health station offering any data you want on your children, yourself, your spouse, or your parents. This impressive mass of information at your disposal will serve to keep you up to date on your health–or to scare the daylights out of you, depending on your frame of mind.

Such technology will also indicate to residents events such as the presence of intruders in the house, a broken window, a leak in the roof, flooding in the basement, a hole in the wall, cockroaches in the kitchen, rats or ants in the attic, and so on. Whatever you wish to know will be detected, recorded, and reported. Bill Gates advocates sophisticated, evolving technology, but which doesn't take priority over everything else. Technology, he asserts, should be easy to use and not too unwieldy. In the future, people will have remote control over their immediate environment. There will be a console in every room, which we will play the way we would on any keyboard. It will be unobtrusively present. An information system must be easy to use–so easy that you use it without even thinking.

We are in a state of transition, a period in which we are exploring and taming the vast field of knowledge opened up by the new infor-

mation technology. The pace of change in this technology is one of the
key factors in the instability that characterizes the present era.

Technological breakthroughs are occurring faster than they can be
marketed, and faster even than people can adjust to them.

Rapid, efficient adoption of the new technology will play a decisive
role in how well companies fare in global competition. Starting right
now, we have to come up with tools that help us to incorporate such
technology into our operations. The United States owes its favorable
position on the global checkerboard largely to the head-start it has
achieved in this field.

A Paradigm for Every Era

This change is as momentous as the advent of printing once was.

Let's take a quick glance back at history. It was the printing press
that allowed for the bible to be widely read. Such uncensored reading
was the crucible in which Luther's Protestant Reformation was born.
As Max Weber convincingly demonstrated, there is a close correlation
between the rise of Protestantism and the development of capitalism.

By extrapolating from this observation, we can assume that a similar
relationship to information will make possible equally significant
changes in our current system of production.

The transition period we are now experiencing is located somewhere between two paradigms, one of which is not quite dead and the
other of which is in its birth pangs.

The industrial era was associated with a paradigm marked by the
production of material goods, by an extremely hierarchical fabric of
social and organizational relations with many intermediate levels, by
isolated, highly regulated domestic markets, by relatively loyal consumers under the sway of both mass marketing and clear-cut, powerful
ideologies borne of a bipolar world.

The information and image era that is already emerging is associated
with a new paradigm characterized by the production of meaning (the
knowledge economy); by an almost "neuronal" fabric of social and
organizational relations with few intermediate levels; by a totally open,
more loosely regulated global marketplace; by consumers with a growing "zap" mentality who are eager for increasingly customized products that require narrower niche marketing; and by the waning of ideological "dogmas" in a multipolar world (since the collapse of the Soviet
Union) that is by now totally interconnected.

THE EVOLUTION OF ORGANIZATIONAL SYSTEMS

Era	Culture	Management	Structure	System
Hunting/ Gathering	Fusion (instinct)	Weld ; fascinate	Informal band	Closed
Agriculture/ Animal Husbandry	Caste (analogy)	Prioritize ; impose	Pyramid	Formal ; mechanistic
Industry/ Commerce	Equality (logic)	Adapt ; negotiate	Inverse pyramid	Deductive ; reactive
Creation/ Communication	Complexity (creativity)	Prompt ; encourage	Interactive cells	Inspired ; proactive

In the current period of blurred borderlines and uncertainty, one in which a new balance has yet to be achieved, everything is in constant, rapid flux. Familiar to physicists, such a state of imbalance is characteristic of transition periods in phases of transformation of matter (from solid to liquid form, then from liquid to gas form).

Our society in transition has an "emotile"
character.

The well-known consultant Edith Wiener has offered an extremely interesting definition of our society in transition which we wholeheartedly endorse. According to her, the society in which we are living is "emotile," an adjective coined on the basis of two major observations.

• The importance of emotion and the search for meaning, which involves a return to a whole range of emotional concerns, including well-being.

• The "motile" component, which suggests perpetual motion, agitation, fleeting conditions.

When combined, these two concepts, which are salient features of contemporary society, suffuse our lives with an *emotile* content. Thus, our yearning for spirituality, our family values, our sense of community, our choices, and our tastes, all of which represent key aspects of every person's identity and behavior, go through emotile stages of varying intensity.

Separating Useful Information From Fatal Information

The Intelligent Use of Knowledge

As soon as we attempt to picture the flood of data and knowledge submerging any organization today, it becomes abundantly clear that we have to build channels and dams to keep this information from flowing out of control and to make it usable.

In the broadest sense of the term, information is nothing but an endless sea of digital bits, each one able to characterize an elementary piece of information–whether it be text, image, or sound–that can be readily differentiated and restored, owing to the power of microprocessors. Furthermore, access to the various media (press, radio, TV) is now concentrated within a single medium which is aptly referred to as multimedia. What we now call "cyberspace" frees us in fact from space and time. Within the next five years, the PCs of roughly half the population in the industrialized countries (whether in private or business life) will be interconnected, thus exacerbating the competition between all existing means of news communication.

A basic assumption underlying all economic models is that our assets are measurable, tangible, and knowable. Yet if the upcoming period is indeed dominated by the knowledge economy, based on the intelligent use of information, then we are heading toward totally intangible, impalpable values that make up what Edith Wiener calls the "nano-environment," one shifting so fast that it cannot be grasped.

We must endeavor to understand the vast number of trends currently reshaping the world–something, however, for which we always seem to have too little time. Today's changes outstrip our ability to conceptualize them.

Hunting for Information, Anywhere, Any Time

Let's consider the example of a company that has succeeded in setting up a particularly effective information collecting system.

EXAMPLE

■ A SMALL, JAPANESE CLOTHING firm manages to turn out ten collections a year comprising 500 models, as opposed to a yearly average of 100 models in the garment industry as a whole. The company's "brain center" is composed of about ten designers. These in-house stylists design all the models and regularly create new forms–without really creating them! The company makes no secret of its guiding philosophy. Since, by definition, fashion involves constantly starting over again, the goal is not to create, but to adapt, transpose, and develop ideas already worked out by others. Essential to this strategy is keeping up on all new market trends as soon as they emerge and being able to grasp whatever similarities they may have with previously existing trends. In this way, cycles can be distinguished. Although former fashions resurface, they always do so with a slight difference, since the fabrics, colors, and accessories change each time. Tokyo Blues sometimes enhances existing models, while at other times simplifying them.

The firm possesses complete, well-organized files on its main competitors, both Japanese and foreign, some of which go back to the 1940s and 1950s. In addition, its collection of French and English fashion magazines runs all the way back to 1860, and even, albeit with more gaps, to 1800. The company's rarest document is a series of fashion etchings that came out at the time of the French Consulate (i.e. between 1799 and 1804).

Owing to its efficiently organized documentation center, the firm has succeeded in creating a kind of information-creation feedback loop, with the ideas of the house stylists or competitors providing the system with constant inputs. Such data is not merely collected, but also effectively analyzed, stored, distributed, and used.

The striking thing about this example is that the creativity of others is rationally exploited through intelligent, systematic use of information. The stylists can look up a collection or model by manufacturer, by year, by season, by stylist, even by theme, picking out forms, patterns, color schemes, and fabric textures from their catalogue. Whenever a trend emerges, they can immediately find out what has already been done along the same lines, in either the recent or the distant past. The stage is thus set for what follows.

With this intelligent way of organizing information, of leaving no stone unturned, of making full use of history and memory, the company always stays one step ahead. It never gets caught napping.

In Japan, the task of collecting data takes on global, and not merely local scope. Firms benefit from the work of "observation posts" set up on the various markets that interest them. The large international trading companies known as *sogo-shoshas* represent, in a sense, the "eyes and ears" of Japanese firms abroad.

Their foreign competitors are quick to denounce this effort as industrial espionage, although the information involved is almost always gathered by open, perfectly legal means. On behalf of their clients, the *sogo-shoshas* carry out what is known in marketing circles as "desk research," i.e. gathering information that has been published or that is available to anyone who requests it, including articles and photos from the press as well as catalogues and price lists of competitors. They derive their strength form the ongoing, systematic character of this work. And although they charge high fees for the service they offer, medium-sized firms can still afford it.

Information thus turns out to be the ultimate weapon. Tokyo Blues merely makes masterly use of an essential tenet of marketing, i.e. information must be the starting point for any undertaking, and the basis for any decision.

Although we are familiar with systematic data gathering, we fail to do enough of it.

This elementary principle of management and marketing is well known, but all too rarely applied. To contemporary managers, there is nothing novel about the need for creativity, for conquest of foreign markets, for experimental thinking, for data gathering and processing.

EXAMPLE

■ **A GOOD MANY HIGH-RANKING PEOPLE AT SYNTHELABO** spend two or three hours a day reading in order to keep up on current trends.

It isn't enough, however, to be acquainted with such principles. You also have to support them actively, apply them with a mixture of imagination and rigor, and instil this mind-set into the entire company. To this end, increasing attention should be paid to potential sources and uses of knowledge throughout the organization. Knowledge is often stored in places where you might not expect to find it. For example, a company must always carefully weigh the advantages and drawbacks of a centralized R & D unit, as opposed to setting up a whole series of smaller labs that are hopefully more in touch with the firm's various lines of business.

Managing Information Means Decoding Information

Adapting to this situation of exponential development calls for constant learning and perfect mastery of the new information systems. This entails several requirements.

1. Managing information flows and overloads.

2. Managing the danger of having truly vital information pushed out by useless information.

3. Promoting interactive use of unprocessed data.

4. Developing systems for filtering, regulating, analyzing, and assessing information.

In order to reach the heart of human knowledge, you have to find a way to work information like a raw material, instead of accepting it as a finished product. Since it is still unprocessed, it must first be refracted through the prism of human qualities. Information should feed knowledge, rather than muddling or stifling it–particularly because it is exceedingly hard for a company to make head or tail of the multiple sources and "noises" that it continually receives.

■ **THE USE OF INTERNET** has already brought about fundamental change in all jobs related to education. At Harvard, millions of dollars have been invested for the purpose of transforming teaching. The aim is no longer to transfer knowledge, but to figure out how to use such knowledge. The professor's task, which used to be imparting information, now revolves around learning how to manage and evaluate information.

This new awareness has given rise to processes for storing and rationalizing information. Once all the information collected has been stored, ordered, and sorted, the task at hand is to use and apply it.

How can companies appropriate all the accumulated knowledge?

In order to enable everyone in the company to make full use of the knowledge available to him or her, to appropriate it, it seems desirable to encourage non-conformist approaches. For example, a substantial percentage of everyone's time could be set aside for learning. 3M applies a 15/85% rule, meaning that every worker is allowed to devote 15% of his or her time to activities of his or her choice, so as to stimulate creativity. Holding inter-disciplinary training sessions and investing in technology transfer are additional methods conducive to spreading knowledge throughout the organization.

If information is pollen, then useful knowledge is honey.

Like a beehive, which transforms the pollen brought in by bees and stores their honey, a company must appropriate information and transform it into knowledge. At the same time, however, it should be borne in mind that only a fraction of the accumulated data will constitute knowledge with any real relevance to an entrepreneurial project.

Organizing Around the Circulation of Information: "Organware," or the Learning Organization

The high-performance model of organization so vital to business success in a period of accelerated change can be summarized as follows.

• Maintaining flexibility and quick reaction time to shifts in the environment.

• Replacing academic conferences with short seminars.

• Making sure that the right people participate, even if they are of lower rank in the organization.

• Setting up matrix structures or constantly renewed *ad hoc* teams in order to promote the activity of both specialists and people with broad-based general knowledge.

• Rewarding those who cultivate relevant knowledge.

• Holding meetings, in the course of work on a project, that bring together experts, involve all appropriate disciplines, and define the necessary processes.[1]

Information must be located at the heart of the organization.

The idea of an organization whose success does not hinge on technology and information has become inconceivable.

Flexible production now makes it possible to turn out small batches of customized products at competitive cost and with remarkable speed. In this fashion, companies establish a new kind of partnership with both their customers and their suppliers. After rendering the notion of mass production irrevocably obsolete, information technology will soon also contribute to redesigning and reinventing a number of industries, starting with the media, banking, insurance, and retail trade.

Information: More a Matter of Sharing than of Exchanging

From now on, the crucial asset will be mastery of information, the raw material of the twenty-first century. The distinctive feature of this resource, however, is that it isn't exchanged; it's rather shared. The underlying logic at work will therefore be completely different.

Failure to understand the importance of sharing in the way in which information circulates may greatly hinder companies, or even organizations of whatever kind.

Information as the Company's Lifeblood

Information is the lifeblood of any company, and many a disease can be traced back to poor circulation. Symptoms include weak per-

---

1. Based on a conference given at Stanford University by William Passemore, "Towards a Syntony of Organware."

ception at all levels of the strategic importance of information; insufficient time for studying available literature; lack of faith in the quality of the information provided (especially if it comes from So-and-so); disregard for the perishable quality of information; discrepancies between the information received at time T and its actual relevance at time $T + n$; information already familiar to the people receiving it.

> *When information is considered synonymous with power, people attempt to hoard it.*

According to Michel Saloff-Coste, the president of the consulting firm MSC, the problem often results from confusion between what is a key resource and the way in which it circulates. Every major stage in economic history, he points out, has its own tools, its own vision of what constitutes power, and its own patterns of organization. Thus, the dysfunctions we observe today can be explained by the tendency of companies operating in the communications age to react in ways appropriate to the agricultural age.

Information is often conceived of in territorial terms because of the gap between the nature of information and the way in which it is culturally integrated. Information cannot be held like land (as in the agricultural mind-set) for the simple reason that it is in constant flux. Unlike land, the more it is disseminated, the greater its value is, whereas it loses value when we jealously hoard it. Information that is not enriched soon becomes obsolete.

EXAMPLE

■ By designing a "browser" for guiding users around the World Wide Web (or WWB), Netscape is already enjoying phenomenal success, since it helps to provide information in a targeted way.

Learning Together

The key element to be taken into account is the transition from a society of survival to a society of individual fulfillment. The paradoxical side of this is that it can only be achieved through serious thinking about group work.

We would like to stress how vital it is to improve the processes involved (a point to which we will return in Chapter 7). This has led us to the conclusion that learning together is conducive to regular upgrades in knowledge and to greater syntony in the company's "organware."

Team work maximizes the exchange of
information.

Today's firm must be a learning organization, one that is able to harness the intelligence and energy of all of its people. To accomplish this task, it must do what is needed for its teams to learn together. Such collective learning has become more essential than ever before for any company that wants to seize the future and escape from mere management based on past experience.

It is on the basis of this perspective that we should consider the virtues of dialogue inside companies.

Freeing dialogue from the dead weight of
power.

As the renowned consultant Manfred Mack put it, "True dialogue enables us to move down from the codified to the non-codified." Socratic dialogue, that age-old but, unfortunately, forgotten practice, makes for mutual enrichment. We should not, however, close our eyes to the rules of the game and the power relations that often distort dialogue. This is why it is so important to establish trust and confidence.

For example, how do we generate effective discussion on specific problems or on the basis of the data collected? The process often seems to be blocked at the level of middle management. Consequently, there exists a huge gap between the knowledge a company can potentially assimilate and the knowledge that is actually available and usable.

The notion that the development of human qualities represents the driving force behind innovation and business success points the way toward a radical shift in management style, one that makes it possible to go beyond the conventional boundaries inside companies. Such a style revolves around the logic of networking. This translates in practice into alliances with other firms for the purpose of mutual aid in the field of information.

Only a climate of trust can protect such new organizations from being overwhelmed by the growing complexity of the environment.

EXAMPLE

- **TEAM WORK IS ONE OF THE KEYS TO THE MANAGERIAL STYLE** of the Japanese clothing firm described above. The owner chooses to work together with his employees rather than to work in isolation. As a result, everyone knows what others are doing, which facilitates communication and makes information travel faster.

---

*Work groups should be formed in such a way
as to facilitate feedback.*

Just how to set up a learning organization is by no means self-evident, however. Too often, we submit conflicts to distant, higher levels in the hierarchy in the hope that they will settle them for us. The danger that lurks is that of inner-company politics. As they grow, companies become increasingly bureaucratic, giving rise to new, intermediate levels, a trend that sometimes has a distorting effecting on information. The practice of withholding, or even wilfully misrepresenting, information may induce senior management to make decisions that are no longer relevant to a changing reality.

It is therefore essential to make sure both that information circulates properly and that there is objective feedback on it. This is why careful attention must be paid to the way in which groups are constituted. Bringing the right people together is often what makes all the difference.

Thus, there are three keys to success that should be borne in mind: asking the right questions from the start, forming teams with great care (usually interdisciplinary teams), and bringing in the appropriate experts. The goal is not so much to provide a tangible solution to a given problem as to encourage all the participants to think together about the problem at hand and to absorb the analyses presented.

Managers should take as much time as needed.

Acting before learning means hindering the development of knowledge. Management often exerts pressure to act when it hopes to get quick results.

It may seem to make sense to want to find a solution as fast as possible in order to meet a deadline or to ward off attacks by competitors. In many such emergency situations, however, the problem is dealt with on the basis of insufficient knowledge, since the people involved haven't taken the time to appropriate the relevant information. Managers must get into the habit of taking as much time as needed.

The point is to strike a proper balance between priorities such as performing on schedule and developing knowledge, to stop thinking that "There will be more than enough time later for learning," an attitude that leads to an exclusive focus on the short term.

*We have to go beyond specialization and foster
individual fulfillment.*

Excessive specialization gradually brings about a situation in which people start going around in circles and in which the company's well of creativity tends to "dry up." It turns out, in fact, that working with a wide variety of technologies can be extremely beneficial. That is why people with a broad educational background can be so valuable.

At present, workers in their 30s and 40s with lots of higher degrees are being called upon to engage in team work, which some of them are practically incapable of doing. Those who had greater inclination for this kind of activity were often pushed out earlier on, owing to the tendency of firms to hire the candidates with the most diplomas. Today's business environment, however, is one of creative complexity that makes it essential to generate diversity, to build a culture of personal fulfillment, teeming with energy and ideas. In this case, nurturing diversity, which is a hallmark of the living world, means recruiting and accommodating talent of all kinds.

A company with a strong culture must be capable of resisting the "clone syndrome," i.e. capable of giving priority to differentiation rather than to promotion of those who appear to have the house profile. Furthermore, all company members should be encouraged to express their own creativity, to be themselves. There are no magic formulas, evaluation grids, or matrixes for achieving this. It all boils down to a change in outlook.

It may seem paradoxical, but the real strength of the Japanese is to avoid falling into purely routine work. They always combine productive gestures with a concern for expanding knowledge. As past masters at storing information and reorganizing it in order to make better use of it, the Japanese display their creativity more in improving techniques and products than in actually designing them.

EXAMPLE

■ **THE JAPANESE NOT ONLY COPIED** the American F-15 plane; they also improved upon it. The Japanese model is lighter and more efficient than the American original.

To conclude, we consider it more stimulating for a company to expand the scope of knowledge of its people. The more we succeed in setting up interdisciplinary teams, the more each participant enriches his or her field of activity. Company members should be induced to give serious thought to the shifts occurring inside the organization, so that they themselves will be in favor of them.

A company that fails to evolve is on its way out.

CHANGE OR PERISH

5

The changes that companies currently have to decode, anticipate, and master are both numerous and weighty. To sail on such turbulent waters, we need a new cognitive map that can replace our older, far too linear, out-of-date maps. We must go beyond our reductionist approach to develop a non-mechanistic vision of human life, to accept the irreducible uncertainty of the universe, as quantum physics already has.

The future has become a moving target. Projections made on the basis of past behavior or strategies are unlikely to be adequate to the task. Dramatic breaks are occurring in all areas–technology, economy, and society. When it comes to getting a handle on the future, uncertainty and complexity are the two new parameters to be taken into account.

We need a tool that fits in with this willingness to accept uncertainty and that enables us to incorporate this approach into our thinking. Such a tool should help us forge ahead in a complex universe characterized by a growing mass of data and by increasingly indissociable, intertwined relations between the various players. It should help us juggle with all these elements by means of an interdisciplinary approach. The tool we are talking about is *competitive intelligence.*

But how do you go about stimulating an urge for competitive intelligence inside the company? As we shall soon see, this notion is inextricably bound up with the will to change, to reengineer the company so that it can adopt new ways of thinking.

The Need for a New Logic to Face the Future

To quote Peter Drucker's famous phrase, "The most dangerous thing in a period of turbulence is not the turbulence in and of itself, but reacting to it with yesterday's logic." If we want to keep growing in a period of upheaval, we have to change paradigms.

How can we get our bearings in this new world and identify its underlying logic? Is there such a thing as a logic of uncertainty? It seems that in the future, things will be "softer," more flexible, more mobile, more oriented toward markets and services. They may no longer fit in with a rigid model.

For example, Taylorism clearly worked wonders for many years in the handling of simple problems. A change in basic data, however, also requires a change in logic.

Einstein once said, "The A-bomb has changed everything except our way of thinking." Much the same could be said today of globalization or information technology. Although they have revolutionized our world, our way of thinking has remained largely stationary.

Past advances in science occurred as a result of shifts in paradigm.

In his work, Einstein endeavored to do the opposite, i.e. to develop a new way of thinking to solve problems. Businesspeople should ponder over this example from the world of science and its implications for their own work.

Scientific discoveries, combined with the most advanced technology, have made it possible to create revolutionary products. Yet what is more important than their actual applications is that these discoveries compelled scientists to conduct a thorough overhaul of established ideas.

This is particularly true of the invisible world of atoms. Quantum physics and relativity helped to modify the classical vision of the world that had held sway since Newton's time. The conceptual upheaval that followed the breakthroughs in quantum physics and relativity have yet to be adequately perceived, much less understood. Although this new vision flew in the face of conformist pressures, no one could question the discoveries associated with it. Whether consciously or unconsciously, engineers and scientists have applied the laws of the new physics in a wide variety of areas, including computers, VCRs, microwave ovens, communications satellites, robotics, and lasers.

A new balance is often preceded by a period of chaos.

In a CD player, a laser is what makes the high fidelity system possible. It reads the microscopic code on the disk, using a procedure that excites light in a crystal. When a laser beam reaches the critical point, the rules of the game change dramatically. Light goes from its initial, chaotic state to a highly ordered, coherent state, thus creating the possibility of reading a microscopic code on a disk with a top-quality, high-fidelity sound. Ordinary light that has not gone through this transition could never equal such a performance.

An interesting analogy may be drawn with the situation of today's companies. Nothing has been as decisive in changing the way firms operate as the break produced by the new information technology. A large number of operations, especially repetitive tasks like inventory control, bookkeeping, and administration have been modified, facilitated, accelerated, and made more reliable than before.

At first, introduction of the new technology was accompanied by a drop in productivity, because companies were still functioning according to traditional patterns that were not conducive to change. This experience provides a striking example of inadequate competitive intelligence. Any company carefully monitoring the environment would certainly have been able to detect the weak signals foreshadowing the breaks–as well as decisive opportunities–to come.

Yet with only a few exceptions, the human community has shown little awareness or comprehension of the conceptual upheaval brought about by these major scientific breakthroughs. Fundamental contributions to this new vision of the world were at first ignored, only to be fully assimilated and utilized much later–a costly delay in terms of time and money.

As Nobel Prize-winner Arno Penzias has pointed out in this respect, "Beyond the invention that precedes innovation, there is a decisive factor–integration. The technologies used in faxes, mobile telephones, memory chip cards, and modems existed long before such products came to market. It was only when the communication problems between the various players involved in integrating the technologies had been ironed out that the market explosion could take place."

In the course of history, science has made available a large number of elements and processes capable of transforming our vision of the world. All too often, we take advantage of them only belatedly.

In the present era, major technological innovations are like warning lights indicating the need for change. This time around, it would be a good idea to take them seriously right from the start.

EXAMPLE

■ **THE AIRCRAFT COMPANY MACDONNEL DOUGLAS** failed to join the jet engine revolution in time. Unable to catch up, the firm was finally bought out by Bœing.

In the present period of turmoil, being aware of the breaks that are coming–or that have already started–before your competitors are is of the utmost importance.

■ ONE COMPANY MONITORING THE MEDICAL FIELD can detect the signs of new breakthroughs four weeks before the innovations officially come out.

In such an environment, shaping the future becomes increasingly difficult. As a result, we tend to focus on the short term, since we feel that we can't have much influence beyond this limited horizon. All this is quite understandable. It is virtually impossible to predict where the world is heading right in the middle of the transition from one epoch to another. We can, however, pay close attention to the upheavals going on in order to be able to gather a few useful clues.

Using the Outside to Change the Inside

Systems theory has made us aware that a company, like any other system, is a network of interacting forces. Like any living organism, it is constantly in danger of degenerating, especially because the "inside" of most firms proves to be inherently conservative. In the absence of outside stimuli, whether contributions or disruptions, systems tend toward homeostasis, i.e. equilibrium. The trouble is that in an unstable environment, equilibrium can spell doom.

The greatest danger facing the system constituted by a company does not come from abrupt change, which takes the form of an immediately perceptible, healthy shock, but from incremental, or even imperceptible change that makes little or no impression.

A shock can serve to wake us up.

It sometimes takes a shock for evolution to occur. The cognitive sciences have demonstrated that a sudden break can help us to grasp previously ignored or unknown facets of reality.

■ **THREE SHOCKS WERE BEHIND MASSIVE RETHINKING AT THE SWISS
FIRM CIBA GEIGY:** a fire at one of the factories, the Bhopal disaster,
and finally Chernobyl.[1] These events forced company members to
realize that after the thousands of deaths involved, the world would
no longer be the same. It was like an electroshock that challenged
their very world view. By raising serious ethical and environmental
questions, the three catastrophes rattled the company's economic
and financial vision.

Eager to identify the leading sources of change that might affect
his firm's various lines of business, CEO Heini Lippuner consulted
futurologist Harlan Cleveland, who brought to light a number of
trends.

1. Major change in the area of information technology.

2. The spectacular development of life science.

3. Significant shifts in values. With the declining influence of
religion, there is a growing concern for equity, ethics, and ecology
that is leading to the emergence of new ideas.

4. Lastly, cultural pluralism, multiple identities and preferences,
and the dilution of responsibility. What does it mean, in such a
context, to belong to a group?

This list made it possible to single out several potential cleavages
between the values of Ciba Geigy and the values of the rest of
society. In such a case, society's values represent a threat to the
company. As a result of this diagnosis, top management initiated a
large-scale process of questioning that proved to be highly beneficial
to the whole company.

Scouts from the Outside

All too often, then, companies need to be jolted before they can
change. Let's consider a more recent example.

■ **A FIRE AT THE FRENCH BANK CREDIT LYONNAIS** made it possible
to "burn down the barriers" between company members. It seems
that the emotional shock caused by the fire at the bank's headquar-

---

1. This example was provided to us at a conference by Mr. Heini Lippuner, Chairman
of the firm's Executive Committee.

ters, a building with immense symbolic value, brought about a considerable shift in the way in which people perceived their work. The result was fewer demands, greater flexibility, and thorough-going architectural rehaul of office space. In a word, the sudden disappearance of the workplace that everyone was accustomed to triggered profound psychological changes.

The problem, however, is that salutary shocks may never occur. This is why it can be useful to get outside assistance. When it comes to competitive intelligence, we need to call upon the appropriate service firms. For certain aspects of their scanning work, they should be connected to think tanks and outstanding personalities who are able to make brilliant syntheses and to give companies greater awareness of the global environment in which they operate.

A number of names immediately come to mind, including Gary Hamel, Rudi Dornbusch, Harlan Cleveland, the members of the Global Business Network (GBN), Rajat Gupta, Paul Hawken, George Stalk, and Peter Haven. All these experts display a stunning capacity for comprehensive and, above all, usable analysis. They can draw attention to forces for change that we might never even have suspected, or that we have failed to take into account because our thinking remains trapped inside the microcosm of a single company.

In fact, however, this microcosm depends on a global macrocosm containing a vast number of components that are likely to influence all areas of competitive activity. Making use of scouts, experts, and distinguished personalities introduces fresh ideas which, however unsettling they may seem, help businesspeople to look beyond their usual frame of reference. Such help offers us a vision or enables us to uncover obvious points that had remained hidden from view. Outside guides (provided they are competent) should be consulted periodically, so that we can keep our eye on the new values that are radically transforming the established business environment.

Nothing changes from the inside.

In addition to shocks that jolt us to a higher level of awareness, there exist more insidious changes that companies may not be able to perceive. As we already pointed out, a system must be shaken up in order to avoid homeostasis. The real challenge for a company that has engaged in serious competitive intelligence and has thereby become aware of the gap between itself and its environment is regaining focus. This is the right time to take a new look at the company's basic business.

Rethinking the Business–from the Outside

Any competitive advantage today will necessarily be short-lived. Rivalry has become so intense and firms catch up so quickly with regard to new technology that no form of growth is truly sustainable. This intensification raises questions and doubts about our basic lines of business and the very conception we have of professionalism.

Thus, we must regularly review our lines of business and our targets, shifting resources according to the new goals we set. Whereas in our mental models, all our lines of business are based on stable know-how, our know-how is currently in a state of permanent flux that shakes its foundations. Similarly, if our knowledge is not constantly updated, it soon becomes obsolete (*cf.* Ch. 8 on knowledge management).

At present, however, professionalism means anticipating changes to come, detecting–in time–the skills required for mastering the new solutions offered by technological progress, both to us and to our competitors.

This represents a daunting challenge. We are compelled to engage in monitoring activity that extends far beyond the current cultural horizon of most firms.

EXAMPLE

■ ESSILOR, the French optician, stays up on progress in both lens technology and the area of optical medicine and surgery. If medicine discovers some way to slow down the onset of far-sightedness by as much as five years, the company's profit margins might be halved. Thus, Essilor defines itself as a vision corrector, rather than as a manufacturer of glasses and contact lenses. This definition of its business is based on the service offered to customers, instead of on the specific techniques employed. This "market-driven" strategy proves to be vital in a period in which incessant innovation produces rapid turnover in technical solutions.

We are moving from an industrial society to a service society, from mass production and consumption to a highly diversified society in which quality takes precedence over quantity. This transition to quality management is also made necessary by technological, geopolitical, and sociopolitical shifts. We have to come up with solutions that are in keeping with the paradigm of the post-Tayloristic organization, one that balances the values of people with the need for economic efficiency.

EXAMPLE

■ **SHELL** turned the method of scenario building into a kind of ongoing group therapy. This was seen as a way to challenge the mind-set of its employees and thereby to keep from getting bogged down in recipes for success that often prove to be out of date.

Increasingly under attack, today's companies have to create new functions to defend themselves. In the past, we had marketing and human resources. Today, notions as diverse as auditing, overall scanning (in relation to social, competitive, geographic, and geopolitical trends), risk management, lobbying, emergency committees, ethics committees, and environmental committees must become an integral part of any serious effort at competitive intelligence. Surviving in a world of increasingly fierce competition requires continual innovation–at an ever faster rate.

The hardest part of all is asking the right questions.

There is a Chinese adage that says, "It is better to teach people how to fish than to give them fish," which we Westerners interpret to mean, "Instead of thinking for others, you should stimulate them to develop their own ideas."

Before launching into a project, it is essential to formulate the relevant questions and to be wary of conventional wisdom. Clichés should be treated with distrust, since they often lead to erroneous judgments. Introspection is vital to developing accurate knowledge of your strengths and weaknesses. When it comes to competitive intelligence, you should start with yourself. Remember: you have to reason from the outside, while still being part of the internal structure.

Our society, the media in particular, focuses attention on certain issues in such a way as to cover up others that no one wants to face up to. As Nobel Prize-winning economist Maurice Allais has written, "It is only through constant challenges to established truth and through the flourishing of new ideas, suggested by creative intuition, that science can advance. All scientific progress, however, comes up against the tyranny of dominant ideas, those held by the various establishments. The more widespread such ideas are–i.e. the more deeply rooted they are in people's psychology–the harder it is to gain recognition for a new conception, however fruitful it may subsequently prove to be."

It is obviously much easier to swim with the current and to follow dominant fashion. The trouble is that fashion is, by definition, what goes out of fashion, as the short-lived "pins" craze clearly shows. This is why it is vital to be able to ask the right questions, which requires decoding both information and disinformation.

■ **Several American TV manufacturers** were convinced at one point of the need to buy out mahogany furniture companies in order to be able to offer their customers a full living-room package. Meanwhile, their Japanese rivals were busy with what really counts in the television business: miniaturizing their TV sets and improving picture quality (especially with regard to color). As a result, the American firms had to drop out of the race.

The Inertia Barrier

Once the right questions have been asked, however, our troubles are far from over. Answering them properly requires breaking out of the mind-sets that weigh so heavily on our organizations. A mind-set is a widely held outlook that corresponds to our perception of reality.

■ **Should General Motors** still be considered essentially an automobile manufacturer? GM now makes more money on financial engineering than on car sales.

Dispelling preconceived ideas thus becomes the basis for any research into the future.

■ **Although the electronic watch** was invented by Lipp and by the Swiss, it was the Japanese who developed it—with phenomenal success and profits. Fortunately, Swatch put part of the electronic watch's success back in Western hands, but the Swiss nonetheless almost "missed the boat." The reason for this is that the Swiss watch industry had fallen victim to an ossified vision of its business and of how to define excellence.

Pressure from the outside forces you to change.

The prime strategic watchword is therefore *watchfulness.* Yet being aware of the need for change is not enough.

Inside a force field, no force acting in isolation can outweigh the energy produced by the rest of the forces. Sporadic change is therefore always dependent on the "good will" of others. This means that true corporate change–even change that doesn't necessarily affect the company's very structure–cannot take place unless all the company's forces have been mobilized behind it.

You can't change the inside from the inside. The only way to do it is to make use of the outside. In the last analysis, only the outside can render change inevitable and thus justify the changes imposed on the inside.

Competitive intelligence is intimately connected to this approach. As Michel Crozier put it, "Change cannot be decreed." [1] Change is a vital necessity. It is for us to figure out how to move along with it, or perhaps even ahead of it. Outside pressure provides the best way of mobilizing for change, since it is clearly inescapable. This is of course assuming that top management is capable of translating such external pressure into internal reforms and of convincingly demonstrating that they are in everyone's interest.

Changing thus means opening up the company to the outside and, in a sense, letting the outside "seep in." Managers are confronted with the paradoxical situation of having one foot inside the organization and the other one outside of it.

Keeping the Movement for Change Moving

The Need for a Proactive Approach

It has become essential to anticipate danger, not only in order to change course in time, but also to make sure you reach the desired destination. A ship with no lookout, with no clear-cut direction, never docks. As Seneca once said, "No wind is favorable to one who knows not where he is going."

Such an emphasis on understanding the future, on proactive anticipation, is not as common in the business world as is generally assumed. Managers tend to think that when things are going smoothly, they have no need for it, and that when things take a turn for the worse, it's already too late for it to be of much assistance.

It should be stressed, however, that whether we are dealing with the health of an organization or the health of an individual, prevention is

---

1. Michel Crozier, *la Société bloquée* (Seuil, 1995). *Cf.* also André-Yves Portnoff and Arlette Portnoff, ed., *Société bureaucratique contre révolution de l'intelligence* (L'Harmattan, 1994).

usually a lot cheaper than cure. To avoid the necessity of expensive repair work, companies must learn how to look ahead and to invent the future.

Creativity: the Vital Ingredient

We can no longer confine ourselves to managing our past achievements. In a world marked by rapid technological innovation, the major strategic challenge has to do with creativity, the human factor. Today's companies need to generate and develop creativity among their people.

Yet sooner or later, many of them find themselves lacking in creative force. How do you regenerate your firm when past formulas for success seem to have run out of steam?

There is no magic recipe for creativity. You have to find a way to develop your own solutions. It has often been said that the best way to master the future is to invent it yourself. However true this may be, it requires being fully informed on what exists and conducting research in every possible direction, involving a wide variety of disciplines, in order to determine which information from competitors is really necessary.

EXAMPLE

■ THE HISTORY OF CREATIVE WORK AT THE AMERICAN CHEMICAL GIANT DUPONT DE NEMOURS is represented in the diagram below. There are periodic surges of creativity which, owing to the high costs they entail, are then followed by periods of tight management aimed at streamlining all operations. Each major stage of creativity thus gives way to a period of rationalization, until a lack of creativity makes itself felt once again. These alternate movements extend over cycles of between seven and fourteen years.

The new world order vastly increases the number of unknown factors.

What will be the driving force in the economy of the year 2000? What will future life styles be like? What will govern consumers' choices?

Every epoch has its own inner logic. We are currently living in a kind of continual transition. Whereas previous transitional periods have always been recognized as such after the fact, as clearly identifiable stages with a beginning and an end, we are consciously experiencing the present one. Although well aware of the changes occurring,

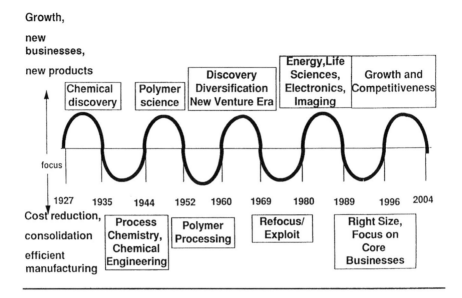

we have a hard time imagining what the end will be like. We can take change into account, but we don't quite know how to deal with it.

In the 1970s, success revolved around freedom and self-expression, whereas in the 1980s, it was more a matter of hedonism and self-absorption. As a result, the 1990s are marked by a growing demand for meaning, by the feeling that something is missing from life.

When we as individuals go through transitions, we don't know where we'll stand in the coming years in terms of income, family situation, the jobs we'll be doing or where we'll be living. Yet even so, we remain consumers capable of making decisions at any given time. Maybe it is up to manufacturers to make a greater effort to take the attendant frustrations and expectations into account, if need be by changing their market offer.

What do we really know in the business world about emerging trends, about reactions to offers in particular areas? In what directions are life styles currently evolving? Are we capable of determining whether something like a global consumer will come into being? Will purchasing patterns change as a result of anxiety over crime, while a kind of "third world" is developing in the ghettos and housing projects of our big cities? What will be the new concerns regarding health, diet, and physical appearance? Where do the future sources of employment lie? How will households be spending their disposable income?

We could go on at length with similar questions, and the list is likely to get longer in the years to come. There is only way for us to be able to answer them: by scanning the environment and attempting to understand what we see. The future is already partially contained in the present, but all too often, a strong signal is perceive to be a weak signal. Once the signal has been minimized, it quickly dies out.

It is vital for us to detect the trends that will affect the ways in which we will be learning, working, and living in the next century. In other words, we need to open our eyes wide.

THE NEED FOR KEEN VISION

6

Scanning as a Core Tool

Scanning the environment is a vital aspect of the process for developing competitive intelligence.

> *Why engage in scanning? To keep your company from suffering the fate of the frog.*

To highlight how essential scanning is to a constantly beleaguered company, let's take a look at a short parable before getting to the heart of the matter: the story of the scalded frog.[1]

There are two possible ways to cook a frog.

1. With the first one, you begin by making sure that neither Brigitte Bardot nor the ecologists are watching, then you throw the cute little creature into a pot full of boiling water. If you choose this method, you'll probably have a hard time achieving what you want, because the frog is going to do everything in its power to get out of the pot.

2. The second one consists of putting the frog in the same pot, while starting out with lukewarm water and gradually increasing the temperature. At first, the frog will feel comfortable; then, it will doze off little by little and let itself get cooked.

Large companies face much the same problem as our frog. If they don't react to changes occurring around them, they may wind up getting boiled. Without realizing it at first, they will gradually lose first

---

1. As told by Peter Senge in *The Fifth Discipline* (Doubleday, 1990), p. 22.

their leadership position, then their competitive advantage, and finally perhaps even their lives as businesses.

An increasingly complex world, one regularly swept by innovation, offers countless opportunities to those who know how to anticipate future trends. However, it can also sink companies that fail to take advantage of these opportunities in time. Admittedly, it isn't always easy to calculate the "return on investment" for such an approach, but failure to adopt it means taking the risk of getting left behind.

In today's environment, only a firm emphasis on scanning can protect companies from slipping gradually into paralysis. The function of scanning is precisely to single out, in the mass of available information, the weak, yet relevant signals that foreshadow the future. The pitfalls to be avoided include the weight of past success (which we have already mentioned), the Wall Street syndrome, and all the problems related to overinformation.

The information you need is within earshot.

Invaluable information lies somewhere inside your business–but never exactly where you need it. One statistical study shows that in large corporations (i.e. with a work force of over 10,000), 80% of all required information can be found inside the company, whatever the subject.[1]

According to some calculations, this proportion has by now risen to nearly 90%. All that it apparently takes is to depart from the usual circuits. The information that companies need in order to gain or maintain a competitive advantage is available right there, without their having to break any laws or violate any ethical precepts.

That many companies fail to make full use of this underlying information, or even ignore it completely, can be explained by the tendency of people to be impervious to signals that are external to their environment or that do not concern them directly. Moreover, people often display a high degree of inertia when it comes to passing information along.

For these reasons, company members all too often act in the following ways.

1. They listen, but fail to pass the information on (classical selfish behavior).

2. They don't listen, but still pass the information on (thereby making it of dubious quality and usefulness).

3. They don't listen, and pass on even less information.

In light of such squandering or retention of information, company leaders need a scanning arrangement involving a set of systems geared

---

1. According to a study conducted by Thomas J. Allen of MIT.

to perceiving, analyzing, and appropriating information. This should enable them to delimit the field of uncertainty, to get partial control over instability, and to attain to a truly global vision of the world and of the changes occurring in it.

The earliest attempts at such scanning activity were a response to the need for assistance felt by corporate leaders. In the process, they formalized what we shall call "the visionary attitude," by helping all key company members to acquire a state of mind conducive to innovation and by making sure that such innovation was in keeping with the deepest aspirations of society.

Sensing the general atmosphere of the times and finding within yourself the means to express it are what make up the inward-looking, mysterious work that forges visionaries.

Detecting Weak Signals

There exists a wide array of weak signals that prefigure future trends, or even radical departures. The goal of a scanning unit is to detect signals that herald crises and opportunities.

These weak signals may be defined as bits of information which can be perceived as such at specific times, but which are usually drowned out by stronger signals. It is the discrete aspect of weak signals in a statistical distribution that prevents them from being detected. Yet when we analyze a crisis or break in retrospect, it turns out that such signals were indeed present, but were simply not perceived and taken into account. In other words, information that had strategic importance for subsequent decisions was left out.

EXAMPLE

■ **FORMS OF KNOW-HOW** developed by companies on the other side of the world can sometimes serve to tip us off. If, for example, a competitor starts applying for a whole series of patents in a particular area, our reflex reaction should be to report this weak signal immediately, since it may attest to a strategic plan to turn the patents into market opportunities at a later stage.

Paying close attention to weak signals from the environment also means keeping up on how they develop over time. If they get gradually stronger, then they are clearly part of a process. If such a process gathers momentum at a time in which the weak signals involved have yet to be perceived or understood, the company will soon find itself lagging behind. François Régnier, who is in charge of studying future trends at Synthélabo, distinguishes three possible scenarios.

1. A weak signal is perceived and made use of in time.

2. A weak signal is neither perceived nor used in time.

3. A strong signal is mistaken for a weak signal and therefore allowed to fade out.

In the present context of mutlifaceted change, any company that wants to avoid drifting off into inertia and defensively clinging to the status quo must therefore conduct scanning activity on all fronts, choosing the right tools and the best available advisors.

This is not, however, all there is to the job of the "lookout" (i.e. someone engaged in scanning). All the collected data, the perceived signals, must then be formalized and communicated to the appropriate company members. Otherwise, instead of being put to good use, the new information will probably wind up collecting dust on someone's shelf.

> *The lookout must be like Buddha–with a*
> *small mouth and large ears.*

Three major features of scanning activity can be distinguished.

1. Scanning must be global and indivisible.

2. Scanning demands methodology so that different information sources can be used with the greatest possible efficiency.

3. Scanning requires organization, in order to promote synergy between the various lookouts.

A lookout must basically adopt the attitude of Buddha, who has a small mouth and large ears.

Thinking Globally, Acting Locally

If we want to go beyond merely apprehending symptoms and understand root causes, we need to engage in systemic thinking. To reflect the relations of interdependence and intertwining that increasingly characterize our world, whether on the micro-level, between disciplines, or on the macro-level, between countries, we can no longer treat problems in isolation. Scanning units must adopt a resolutely comprehensive approach.

Systemic thinking involves studying the connections between disciplines, between entities, between phenomena. What makes this so important is that a company is itself a system, i.e. a whole whose parts interact and are organized to achieve an end.

The Need for Awareness of the Past

Whoever ignores his or her own past will never be able to anticipate future possibilities. By the same token, any company that aims to grasp its future must first understand its own history.

*Failing to see invariant factors means being
blinded by a dogmatic attachment to change.*

We can distinguish two opposing tendencies that in fact represent
symmetrical errors.

• Overestimating the pace of technological change, without recognizing that what is economically profitable may not always be socially
desirable.

• Underestimating the weight of inertia.

It is a mistake to imagine only what might change, without carefully
taking stock of what remains constant.

EXAMPLE

■ **THE OLD BAKERY WHERE YOU BUY YOUR BREAD IN THE MORNING** is
filled with both delicious smells and a particular atmosphere. You
enjoy it because of the way it feels, because of the cosy atmosphere
you find there. A company gets bought out, reorganized, and mod-
ernized. The magic suddenly rubs off, and if the former culture is
not replaced by a new, equally compelling culture, company members become disaffected.

This example calls to mind the competitive mistake made by many
Western companies on East Asian markets. We often fail to understand
that prior to buying our products, Asian investors buy our culture as
well as certain idiosyncrasies deriving from our art of living.

*A company that does insufficient scanning may
soon fall behind.*

In military jargon, the term "intelligence" refers to an activity of
constant watchfulness, of strategic information gathering with the aim
of anticipating threats and thereby preserving the security and integrity
of a nation. Likewise, keeping a close watch on everything our existing
and potential competitors do is a decisive factor in helping us to maintain our competitive edge.

In order to clarify what scanning really is, we will start off by
explaining what it is not. This to avoid confusion with previously
existing techniques, and above all to show how scanning must be
introduced in situations in which conventional companies fail.

Scanning is not an additional form of espionage

It has become vital to study the competition in a serious, consistent
fashion. It simply isn't enough to have your inventions duly patented,

considering how quickly other companies now catch up with technological leaders. For this reason, the aim of competitive intelligence is
to set up research units able to monitor on an ongoing basis the strategies of competitors, as well as to rethink and overhaul R & D policies.

From the black approach (spying) to the white
approach (scanning).

Needless to say, there also exist dubious ways of observing what
competitors do, as opposed to honorable, legitimate scanning methods.

To maintain—or to gain—a competitive edge, some companies will
stop at nothing. In order to anticipate their rivals' next moves, they may
even make use of former, bona fide spies who snoop around in ways
that frequently fly in the face of the law or of elementary business
ethics. Given this negative image, many companies shy away altogether
from the idea of competitive intelligence. They would rather accept
things passively than engage in controversial activities that are often
rightly condemned.

There exists a certain gradation in intelligence efforts.[1]

• The *white approach* refers to competitive intelligence in the sense
that we use the term in this book.

• The *grey approach* refers to competitive snooping, a tool to be
wielded with caution.

• The *black approach* refers to out-and-out industrial espionage,
which we consider reprehensible.

Some companies that have trouble getting the white approach to
work for them may panic and engage in industrial espionage, adopting
methods pioneered by the secret services around the world. After all,
they reason, the very concept of competitive intelligence derives from
the world of military strategy.

We will now endeavor to characterize these three approaches.

The black approach is out-and-out industrial
espionage.

This specter, which seems to come straight out of a James Bond
movie, is unfortunately also part of reality. A number of secret services
have redeployed themselves in industrial espionage. In a context of
increasingly relentless competition, some companies now feel that
there are no holds barred.

The fact of the matter is that large amounts of money can be saved
through spying. Far from declining, illicit methods of obtaining information are currently enjoying a boom on the world market, in a context

---

1. See Pierre Cadet, *Pour agir et animer autrement dans une société en mutation* (Éditions Cabi, 1994).

in which the number of available henchmen has risen exponentially and in which the Sicilian Mafia has new, up-and-coming competitors from Eastern Europe, who are branching out westward.

This regrettable distortion of an otherwise respectable concept serves to highlight just how necessary true competitive intelligence is. How do we dissociate our scanning activity from industrial espionage, with which it is all too often equated? The answer is disarmingly simple: an activity may be considered industrial espionage if it involves breaking the law. Some methods are clearly illegal, such as hunting down classified defense secrets or information on the private lives of competitors (through wire-taps, bribery, forgery and the use of forgery, etc.). In contrast, others–consulting the press and data bases, conducting interviews, cultivating widespread business relations–are perfectly lawful and legitimate.

When necessary information is not available, there are powerful techniques of analysis (validating assumptions, ferreting out contradictions) that make it possible to piece the puzzle together and to get a fairly faithful image of the real situation. In addition to public information, there are means to gaining access to more confidential sources, while remaining within the bounds of law and ethics.

The definition of espionage in the new [French] penal code is so vague that it could include any exchange of information between France and a foreign country (the Americans have voted equally imprecise laws). For this reason, trade associations like the SCIP (Societies of Competitive Intelligence Professionals, which boasts 4,000 members from a dozen different countries) are working to establish codes of ethics that give professionals a clear framework within which they can work.[1]

Moreover, the mere desire to harm competitors sometimes leads companies to spread viruses in the computer systems of their rivals– a trick that is widespread and getting more so all the time. These invisible viruses affect the way in which software functions, either modifying the contents of programs or even totally destroying them.

Another sensitive area is Internet, which offers a fabulous, free arena in which everyone can not only have access to the knowledge developed by humanity, but also participate in creating it. What was once a forum enabling research workers to exchange ideas has become a virtual battlefield for governments, companies, and gurus from around the world. The question of how to regulate Internet is now a more burning issue than ever before. In Russia and France, cryptography is already being used to protect confidential information.

---

1. Interview in the Paris newspaper *Libération* (May 15, 1995) with Yves-Michel Marti, who is the author of *l'Intelligence économique: Les yeux et les oreilles de l'entreprise* (Éditions d'Organisation, 1995).

The grey approach, or competitive intelligence
that bends the law.

On highly open markets, knowing how your competitors work is of the utmost importance. The following examples present various versions of the grey approach.

• Obtaining information during job interviews with executives formerly employed by competitors.

• Sending a delegation to visit a factory, with each member instructed to carry out a specific task such as "carelessly" dipping a necktie in a liquid the subsequent analysis of which might reveal trade secrets, or wearing sticky-soled shoes that pick up the various dust particles on the floor.

• Paying a headhunter to provide information that is otherwise hard to come by.

Practices of this kind, which border on the illegal and which were typical of earlier times, can be safely abandoned if we settle down to developing an appropriate, entirely legal approach to scanning.

Scanning–the white approach–amounts to a
particular frame of mind.

This methodology implies creating a number of scanning activities on the environment, both global and local, that make it possible to pick up all the weak signals sent out by the competition as well as by the areas of politics, law, ecology, and society.

The white approach consists of detecting and anticipating information, but above all circulating it far and wide, and explaining it so that everyone involved clearly perceives the weak signals transmitted. Lookouts must also be able to facilitate the job of decision-makers, who have little time or energy for monitoring the global environment. They must therefore channel and direct information to people in the field, providing them with material to enrich their decision-making.

THE VARIOUS SOURCES OF INFORMATION AVAILABLE TO COMPANIES

These sources of information may be classified according to their nature and their position in time.

• *Text information.* This kind of information can be recorded in text form that can be managed by computers. This includes internal or external data bases, full texts, etc. Such information represents between 40 and 60% of all available information (e.g. the press, trade publications, and Internet servers).

• *Company information.* This kind of information has to be actively sought outside the company. It includes visits to customers, reports on competitors, and meetings with equipment and materials suppliers. Such information represents between 30 and 60% of all available information (e.g. fact-finding trips, job interviews, and trade negotiations).

• *Expert information.* This kind of information constitutes a large part of any company's memory. The right experts are often right at hand–unbeknownst to us. Managing internal know-how is particularly important in the current period, marked by massive reengineering, relocation abroad, and early retirement. Such information represents between 10 and 20% of all available information (e.g. symposiums, conferences, lectures, and research workshops).

• *Trade show information.* In all lines of business, there are places and events that are particularly conducive to contact between manufacturers, suppliers, research workers, and consumers, where new products are presented. Companies can glean vital information from events like trade shows and open-house days, provided that they carefully prepare for collecting the relevant information.[1]

However, information also possesses a time structure that often affects how useful it is to companies. Information may be historical or relevant only to the immediate present; it may forecast future trends or actively anticipate them.

Information may also be treated differently, depending on the model of capitalism in which it develops (e.g. closed market economies, open market economies, "mixed" market economies).

It is therefore essential to distinguish between the various kinds of information, to arrange it in order of priority, to make sure it is properly collected and assimilated, and to put it in perspective.

Scanning is not a trend toward overinformation

In business as in the rest of life, we are constantly submerged, or even assailed, by tons of information, much of which is largely irrelevant to our day-to-day work. What is worse, it may even serve to conceal other information of vital strategic importance.

There is a world of difference between fatal information, which constitutes the "noise" around us, and useful information, which constitutes the "information signal" with high value that can have con-

---

1. See C. Hunt and V. Zartarian, *Le renseignement stratégique au service de votre entreprise* (Éditions First, Paris, 1990).

siderable impact on overall strategy or specific tactics—as long as it is conveyed to the right person at the right time.

At a wide variety of hierarchical levels in today's companies, a growing number of people complain that they are swamped with "over-information." The ironic thing is that such people often act as though they needed more and more information all the time. It should be noted that this phenomenon occurs more frequently in large corporations with the most forward-looking management practices than in small firms lacking in such sophisticated tools.

The tendency toward overinformation is one of the many facets of modern life. Needless to say, it results from technological progress (e.g. information technology), which makes it both easier and cheaper to process, store, and distribute information. This temporary disorder is characteristic of a period marked by rapid technological change. "Useful" information is in fact the very opposite of "overinformation."

A scanning unit collects useful information, operating like a processing center.

Scanning is a way of reacting to the mass of information a company receives. It serves a relay function, or rather the function of a "processing center."

A good many companies still process information in prehistoric fashion. We should handle information as if it were a precious mineral, identifying deposits, digging it up, sorting it, filtering it, cleaning it, and purifying it. At the end of the whole process, what is left is a small nugget of high-value information.[1]

Scanning is not an additional forecasting tool

Scanning bears no resemblance to any of the conventional models for representing the future. It is the expression of a new world: the emergent world, rather than the certain world.

Different mind-sets lead to apprehend information in different ways. Close observation of behavior in relation to information and decision-making makes it possible to distinguish three basic situations, which illustrate different modes of cognitive perception, different conceptions as to how to manage the future.[2]

1. Excerpt from an interview with Yves-Michel Marti on LCI radio, July 24, 1995.
2. This breakdown into three worlds is presented by Andrèu Solé in an article entitled "La décision: production de possibles et d'impossibles," *in Traité d'ergonomie* (Éditions Octares, Paris, 1996).

*We have moved from a world of certainty to a
world of probability.*

For a long time, our society saw itself as living in a deterministic universe, characterized by the elimination of uncertainty and the reproduction of what previously exists. In this "certain world," information constituted a mirror of reality, and scanning the horizon was not felt to be necessary. This was also the heyday of Taylorism. Within this paradigm, it was assumed that the right information led to the right decisions.

In contrast, the probable world is marked by the *reduction* of uncertainty, by an evolutionary process in relation to what previously exists, and by adjustment to reality. Information is seen as perception, as one of many images of the past, present, and future. This attitude is often likened to what is called "the rear-view mirror effect." We are all accustomed to predicting and envisioning the future on the basis of what we see in our rear-view mirrors, that is, by looking behind us.

In the probable world, information leads us to entertain several different hypotheses. It does not result in *the* right decision, but in several possible ones. This is the world in which today's companies must operate.

*The next step involves moving from the
probable to the emergent.*

Perceiving emergence is the goal toward which we should strive. The emergent world is characterized by the production of uncertainty, by sharp breaks with what previously existed. It even leads to participating in creating the world toward which we are heading. It is at this juncture that scanning comes in, as a way to manage the transition from one world to another.

The emergent world is teeming with the weak signals we described earlier.

In business, the certain world and the probable world involve managing what exists, or at most improving upon what we already know how to do, what we can readily predict. The emergent world is the mental universe in which innovation takes place.

Yet today's companies are the scene of strong pressure to conform that can be traced back to the mind-set of Taylorism. Caught up in day-to-day operations, people often find themselves ill-equipped to pick up the weak signals around them. Furthermore, it is always difficult to convince others of a hunch that has not yet been fully confirmed or validated. We have also seen how the concept of "weak signal" implies a certain duration and thus requires projecting into the future. Lastly, we have observed just how hard it is to make room for this concept in traditional linear, rationalistic models.

In spite of all these difficulties, however, scanning responds to the needs of this third world in business. The two other worlds should now be confined to narrow management tasks.

Scanning is not a means to reduce uncertainty, but to trigger it.

In order to operate within the emergent world, scanning must encourage innovation in such a way as to suffuse all company constituents with it. In fact, in a decision-making process that aims at innovation (e.g. designing a new product), it is not so much information that counts as the decision-makers' "black box," meaning their implicit lines of reasoning (regarding customers, competitors, technology), their certainties, convictions, images, and analogies.

Yet true innovation involves breaking with what exists, and thereby *raising* the level of uncertainty. By contributing to the reduction of uncertainty, information seems to contradict the idea of innovation. It is also a weapon with perverse effects, since it sometimes allows people to make themselves indispensable, to justify themselves after the fact, to protect themselves, and, when push comes to shove, to avoid making decisions. All it takes is to produce, circulate, request, and share an ever increasing mass of information. This makes the situation so "complex" that deciding one way or another ultimately appears to be too risky.

In short, however paradoxical it may sound, information often constitutes an obstacle to decision-making. According to its traditional definition as reduction of uncertainty, information can bring about the direct opposite, i.e. by increasing our cognitive inability to decide–to the point of self-paralysis.

Scanning is a tool for opening up new possibilities.

"Innovating means opening up new possibilities." Insufficiently processed information, however, turns out in most cases to bar possibilities ("The better you know your customers and your market, the fewer possibilities you have."). The role of scanning is to counteract this phenomenon, by serving as a tool for opening up new possibilities.

Decision-makers must choose between several possibilities. The resulting choice unquestionably constitutes one of the key components in the innovation process–provided it isn't hampered by inappropriate use of information.

This, then, is what scanning is not. We have chosen to begin with this aspect of the issue precisely because scanning represents a break with past and, unfortunately, much of present practice in the field of management, forecasting, and adaptation. We are living in a world of the unknown, and being proactive means openly embracing this unknown character. A lookout is someone who, far from fearing the unknown, is willing to dive right in.

In what follows, we will attempt to formalize this creative approach to getting a grip on the unknown.

How to Scan

Although it is important to turn over a new leaf in order to understand and accept scanning, this approach should not be considered some kind of vague catch-all that defies all efforts at formalization or organization. On the contrary, scanning units make ample use of the best available tools for investigation and analysis, while giving free rein to intuition, curiosity, and imagination.

This combination of approaches which the conventional wisdom has always deemed incompatible–rigor and rationality, as opposed to intuition and imagination–can only be achieved through all-out, full-scale observation that breaks free from traditional dichotomies. To this end, we have drawn up a list of seven possible forms of scanning, which seem to us to be the most essential of all.

THE SEVEN FORMS OF SCANNING CONDUCTED AT L'ORÉAL

Societal
Examples:
• Positioning women in the year 2000.
• The effect of the ageing of the population on markets.

Competitive
Examples:
• Competitors' interest in new technology.
• Shifting boundaries between the areas of health, cosmetics, and the food industry.

Geopolitical
Examples:
• Shifting power relations following the collapse of the Eastern bloc.
• The future of NAFTA.

Technological
Examples:
• New molecules developed in the US and Japan.
• Japanese research in biotechnology.
• Ceramic powders.

Market
Example:
New trends in distribution like home shopping.

Legislative
Examples:
The impact of European unification on the field of health.
Declining health-care expenses in Germany.

Geographical
Examples:
Identifying new market opportunities (China, India, etc.).
Finding ways to get through to distant cultures.

Technological Scanning

The term *technological scanning* refers to a company's efforts, the means it uses, and the steps it takes in order to be on the lookout and to detect all changes and innovations emerging in the areas of technology that are relevant to its business, or that might be in the future. This activity involves observing and analysing the scientific, technical, and technological environment as well as its present and future economic implications in order to identify both opportunities for and threats to development.

A number of arguments militate in favor of a methodical approach to technological scanning. Japan's stunning economic success can in large part be attributed to concerted, systematic, painstaking efforts at collecting any and all relevant information published throughout the world. In this respect, technological scanning goes hand in hand with competitive scanning, which will be dealt with in the next section.

Being thoroughly acquainted with competitors' strategies and customers' expectations is not enough. A company must also keep a close watch on research and development activities and technological break-throughs, which may otherwise endanger its very existence. Choosing the right technology at the right time often takes on decisive strategic significance.

The advent of new technologies is gradually accomplishing a radical change in perspective regarding the activities and the resources that shape a company's choices and policies. It is therefore crucial to pay close attention to any major technological break that occurs.

There exist four kinds of breaks.

• Incremental change.

• Radical change based on major, ground-breaking innovations (e.g. the steam engine, the railroads, electricity, oil, information science, and telecommunications).

• Technical revolutions, i.e. innovations specific to each period that transform the industrial process. In the nineteenth century, these include the internal combustion engine and the rotary furnace, which made possible the passage from handicraft to mass production. In the twentieth century, the next shift was from mass production to custom production (microchips, artificial intelligence, new materials).

• Occasional shifts in paradigm, with change occurring at the high-est possible level—that of an entire civilization.

We must carefully monitor such shifts in order to improve our strategic business thinking.

Patents should be analyzed.

The analysis of patents taken out by a company can be highly revealing as to its competitive position. We can deduce from the rising or falling curve of a firm's patent applications whether it is gaining or losing ground to its competitors. In addition, any company applying for a patent is required to mention the patents it used in bringing about its invention.

This kind of analysis is especially useful to high-tech firms, whose competitive standing may change rapidly, and to pharmaceutical com-panies, whose future depends essentially on the quality of their research teams. In these cases, the number of patent applications pro-vides serious clues as to the likely competitive line-up of tomorrow.

When it comes to keeping track of patent applications, we must pay careful attention to attempts at establishing priority rights, and to sub-stitution or improvement strategies, while distinguishing actual research policy from red herrings. It should also be stressed that in spite of all the precautions taken by companies, their patents offer only dubious protection against competitors.

- **CANON** succeeded in undermining Rank Xerox's leadership through an ingenious policy of sidestepping the patents protecting Xerox's photocopy machines, by taking advantage of legal subtleties. As a result, Xerox was unable to prevent its competitor from copying its technology.

Moreover, technological scanning may help a company to avoid wasting resources. For example, many companies make the mistake of investing heavily in Research and Development on products that competitors have already rendered obsolete.

Technological scanning should also, however, be practiced internally. This goes particularly for large-scale firms that are in need of powerful innovations. The following example from 3M offers an interesting illustration of this point. This story should be seen against the backdrop of the company's bold, global vision. Recognized as a world leader in terms of encouraging creativity, 3M takes its commitment to technological scanning to the point of exploiting even the slightest impulse of technical creativity on the part of its employees.

- **3M HAS SOME 45,000 PRODUCTS** in its catalogue, which go through evolution, renewal, and decline. Every division of the company is called upon to achieve at least 30% of its sales on products less than five years old. There is a powerful urge for innovation and R & D that is rooted in the firm's culture, which emphasizes the importance of people and their spirit of initiative. Research workers are therefore not shut up in some ivory tower. If they like, they can always go down to the production lines to keep up on a product they helped to design.

  This breakdown of departmental barriers is symbolized by an annual "creativity fair" open only to 3M employees, which allows for the greatest possible exchange between the various divisions and functions within the corporation. At a visit to a trade show, one of the executives in charge of the 3M investment team got the idea of setting up a similar event reserved for 3M managers from around the world, who could thus get the chance to meet their colleagues from branches in other countries. There would be stands presenting the projects and achievements of each unit.

  The first show of the kind, which was held in 1985, was a tremendous success. Large numbers of 3M people from around the world, from engineers to salespeople, thus got the opportunity to "shop" for technological innovations and to engage in discussion with technical and scientific specialists sent by the various divisions. A good many 3M products developed between twelve and eighteen months later came out of discussions held at the fair.

Competitive Scanning

Competitive pressure forces companies to come up with new sources of competitive advantage all the time. Thus, after developing marketing techniques aimed at improving product reliability and making the sales force more aggressive, after using the lever of motivation techniques in order to stimulate workers' enthusiasm, the most dynamic firms now feel emboldened to attack their competitors head-on, either by practicing benchmarking or by engaging in strategic warfare, which consists of deliberately rendering obsolete the development plans worked out by rival firms.

It would be a mistake, however, to define the competitive environment in an excessively restrictive fashion. On the contrary, competitive scanning should make us aware of the existence of players who, for the time being, are only indirect rivals. There are two major reasons for this.

• The boundaries between different industries are becoming increasingly blurred, a situation that creates a growing number of opportunities located at the point of intersection between industries.

• The new information technology is bound to destabilize certain territories and traditional lines of business.

Calmly observing what competitors are up to requires accurate, consistent management of the signals sent out by the firms in your environment. In this regard, a distinction should be made between tangible analysis and intangible vision.

Tangible Analysis

In competitive analysis, a company starts out by evaluating its performance potential on the basis of its tangible assets. This leads to essential questions.

1. Are our industry and our main product area intrinsically attractive, i.e. structurally profitable in the long run?

2. In the industry thus defined, is the company in a position to achieve adequate performance in comparative terms, i.e. does it have enough assets in relation to its rivals?

Working out a tangible vision may mean using tools like Michael Porter's matrix, which helps to analyze a company's competitive position and the relative attractiveness of its line of business on the basis of who the various players on the market are (suppliers, distributors, substitute products, potential new entrants). It may also, however, involve examining the degree of maturity of the relevant industry, which gives an idea of how stable the economic environment is. Maturity can be measured with the help of the following indicators: the industry's overall growth rate, its potential for expansion, and the evolution of its products and technology.

Tangible analysis of a competitor then requires keeping a close watch on a number of specific factors. They include the competitor's current performance, his strategy, his most recent objectives, his capabilities, the assumptions that appear to underlie his moves, and his decisions.

There are a number of tangible factors that we sometimes fail to observe, but that can nonetheless provide us with valuable information.

• **Accelerating inventory turnover.** How do competitors turn over their stocks? The answer to this question may reveal significant new sources of profit.

• **Improvement of logistical systems.** We have moved from systems for replenishing raw materials to the just-in-time system, thus opening the way to synchronizing production and sales. How can we go even further in this direction? What will the next step be?

• **The entire costing system.** This is often little more than a set of conventional practices. If they hinder competitive strength, then the only way to detect them is through comprehensive scanning.

Beware of conventional cost accounting practices.

Evaluating cost in terms of a specific line of activity is an important aspect of measuring performance. Some large companies are engaged in a wide variety of businesses that are divided up among several independent strategic business units.

What often happens is that costing systems establish company-wide standards that show no recognition of the fact that companies sell highly diversified product lines that call for quite different technologies. As a result, management uses erroneous data to decide on pricing, product mix, raw materials, production technology, and the right response to competitors' products.

Accounting methods are formalized at a given time, with rules that are reapplied year in and year out and that sometimes prove to be ill-suited to a new context. Product lines and distribution channels have undergone fundamental changes in recent years. Labor now represents an increasingly smaller share of a company's overall costs, whereas the cost of marketing, engineering, and information management have skyrocketed.

Although often neglected in competitive scanning, costing systems may reveal unsuspected opportunities. Often, hiring a former employee of your main rival can help you evaluate your costs in relation to those of your competitor, whose costing procedures may well turn out to be more ingenious than yours.

We can therefore evaluate costs on the basis of the kind of activity involved in the following manner.

• Collecting accurate data on labor and materials costs.

• Distinguishing the key items that allow for cost-cutting.

• Bringing to light the resources that are consumed to varying degrees, depending on the product or product line, and seeking alternative supply sources.

• Emphasizing resources that don't always have a correlation with traditional accounting procedures for allocating costs such as labor, production time, and raw materials.

With such an evaluation system, indirect costs (e.g. company-wide overhead) are first divided up among the various businesses, then attributed to the individual products. At this stage, the task is to examine "big budget items" so as to imagine new ways of reducing significant expenses.

In the cosmetics and perfume field, for example, companies can cut unit cost by as much as 50% just by considering issues in a new light, after acquisition of other businesses whose practices in this area are significantly different, but positive. By closely observing how bought-up firms operate, we can find ways to reorganize our own product portfolios.

EXAMPLE

■ IN THE COURSE OF ITS DIVERSIFICATION STRATEGY, a major cosmetics firm discovered on several occasions that the newly acquired businesses had a significantly more advantageous cost structure, particularly as regards the price they paid for packing materials. This discovery led the company to question a number of its long-standing beliefs.

Intangible Vision

Companies usually do a fairly good job in formulating traditional quantitative analysis, because of what is referred to as "the Wall Street syndrome," meaning everything related in one way or another to financial analysis and the reaction of the market. We tend to forget that the kind of financial analysis demanded by the stock market has precious little to say about how well a unit will be able to defend itself and maintain its competitive strength in the future.

Clearly, then, qualitative, soft information is every bit as important as hard data. Businesses like fashion, movies, and advertising, which depend by definition on intangible sources of inspiration, owe their ability to renew themselves to a general, immaterial environment, a vague spirit of the times that they manage to perceive.

A company must also be analyzed in light of its intangible assets, of which we have given a few examples. These assets can have a considerable, often underrated impact on the company's future. Imagine a firm that drastically reduces its advertising budget one year, while its competitors continue to invest heavily. Although in the short run, the firm may still chalk up honorable results, it won't be long before the others start pulling way ahead of it. Another example would be a pharmaceutical company that freezes its research and development spending out of a desire to safeguard short-term profits. Earnings may grow by leaps and bounds, but the company has jeopardized its future.

A company may also show impressive results that were achieved only by sacrificing past loyalty to distributors and customers. In such a case, new product initiatives may fall through, since the firm has forfeited its credibility with consumers.

The intangible factors of today will dictate the
tangible factors of tomorrow.

A company's image can rapidly prove to be out of date. All it takes is for a catalogue to look too old-fashioned or for the company's teams to be insufficiently cohesive. Thus, when acquiring another firm, we have to make sure that its apparent profitability doesn't mask a seriously depleted goodwill.

Some American companies list their brands as balance-sheet assets. A company's collective know-how, the quality of its people, should also be considered in the same way, however difficult it may be to estimate the precise value of skills.

Hard-to-quantify intangibles are part of the frame of mind needed for preparing the future, whereas tangible factors are more clearly associated with the present, or even the past. To achieve acceptable bottom-line results–the results on the basis of which they will be judged–all too many managers make rather dubious decisions such as doing away with advertising, slashing inventory, and placing too heavy a burden on distributors.

Although difficult to quantify, all these intangible factors can still be measured by means of appropriate competitive scanning. The good thing about scanning is precisely that its informal, mutlifaceted character flies in the face of quantitative dogma, which necessarily narrows perspectives. Competitive edge does not always derive from technological advantage, since the news of breakthroughs usually circulates fast enough to enable other companies to catch up in short order.

Smaller firms now have access to significant new technology. It is therefore people that should be placed in the foreground of corporate life. They are the main source of competitive advantage today. It could almost be said that intangible assets foreshadow the long-range value of a company, because they constitute a vital aspect of its identity, and thus of its ability to survive.

The intangible is therefore one of the keys to the future. It used to be enough to create a large technological gap in relation to rivals. From here on in, however, we have to go much further. Distribution systems, relations developed with distributors, customer loyalty, the quality and expertise of creative teams, as well as everything else that concerns human input are the chief sources of competitive advantage.

The most significant intangibles are the following.

• Customers' emotional satisfaction.

• The core skills of the different business units.

• The professionalism shown by the marketing team, the quality of the research staff, the expertise of the finance team, and the achievements of the engineering department.

• The loyalty and commitment of all these teams.

• The strength of the brand image.

• The strength of the corporate image.

• The CEO's charisma.

In the intangible economy, we are faced with several fundamental challenges.

• Deploying an energetic sales strategy predicated on the will to establish high-quality relations with customers.

• Reshaping company policy on the basis of customers' aspirations and criticisms.

• Making research activities and production systems flexible enough to keep up with shifting consumer tastes.

• Placing emphasis on the hybrid couple product-service, which is the only way to add real value to a product.

There seems to be no limit to the directions that competitive scanning can take, apart from the cost of accumulating and processing data.

Of course, the information gathered in this way is highly varied and of uncertain value. Taken in isolation, none of it has much significance. But once we start comparing the data, establishing connections, accumulating and checking information, we can uncover entire areas of a competitor's strategy.

Motivation systems should be taken seriously.

Large corporations that are pitted against smaller, more flexible competitors must make sure that their organizational structure and even their motivation systems are not too far out of line with what is customary in their industry. The idea of establishing uniform, worldwide compensation and motivation systems in order to simplify matters in a multinational firm is simply unrealistic. Business activities may vary widely between the company's branch offices, as may the different local pay scales and motivation systems.

EXAMPLE

- **A LARGE SERVICE COMPANY DOUBLED ITS GROWTH RATE** by reducing the number of profit centers from 30 to 6, shifting from a geographical vision to a functional, international vision of its business, and by making compensation of top executives dependent on the income generated by the various teams and the entire firm, rather than on the profit made by their own units.[1]

If one of your competitors shows greater efficiency in specific areas of the business, it is essential to determine whether this advantage might not derive from a more intelligent motivation system than the one you use.

Should competitive scanning be outsourced?

When seeking to perfect a scanning system, a company may find it helpful to call in a consultancy firm for classifying, organizing, and bringing the assembled data under control—as long as the in-house scanning unit takes charge of formalizing and connecting up all the information.

Such assistance is offered by the Sorgem consulting firm, for example. Using a semiological method of analysis, Sorgem attentively observes all the signals sent out by a company (advertising, packaging, press kits, logos), identifying how often they recur, as a means to reconstituting the company's strategic orientation. In a sense, the consultants engage in an activity reminiscent of the long, fascinating work of entomologists.[2]

Market Scanning

Market scanning can be divided up into several distinct focuses that are all too often ignored, although they contain a wealth of information. For example, effective market scanning enables you to ascertain whether your chief competitor is offering suppliers much better terms than you are.

---

1. This example was provided by Mercer Management.
2. See Christopher Babinet, *Le Devoir de la vigilance* (Éditions Denoël, 1992).

Customers and Markets

The point here is to keep track of the changing needs of customers, their changing relationship to the company, and, to a lesser extent, their solvability. This can lead a company to discover new markets and different, more promising networks. Considering how self-evident this activity sounds, it is surprising how few firms engage in it.

Delivery cost and quality are additional factors that must be taken into account. If competitors deliver the goods twice as fast as you do, the resulting decline in efficiency, however slight it seems, may in the long run have a negative impact on overall corporate results. Likewise, an unsuitable distribution circuit can be of strategic import. The Tak Corporation, a Japanese consulting firm specializing in the field of distribution, attributes the difficulties encountered by a number of Western brands on the Japanese market to mistakes in choosing distribution channels, which were based on Western models that are largely irrelevant to the context in Japan.

Suppliers

The company should also stay informed about the supply of new products, the changing relationship of suppliers to the company, and the suppliers' ability to provide essential products at the lowest possible cost.

Suppliers can help the company in three ways.

• They can stay on the lookout for ways to extend their markets.

• They can inform you as to who provides what to whom. Such information makes it much easier to find out exactly what technologies are being used upstream and downstream from the supplier.

• You can exchange information with your suppliers. They stand to gain from the information you provide them, particularly regarding changes in the suppliers' own markets. Moreover, there are strong grounds for working out a formal arrangement that balances rights and obligations, and that spells out favors to be exchanged.

The Labor Market

The company should also stay abreast of changes in the supply of new skills, in relations between labor and management, and in manpower costs. Close attention should be paid to the desires of young people and the emergence of new areas in training and education.

Dissatisfaction

Last of all, all signs of dissatisfaction should be taken seriously, however minor they may seem. Even if 95% of all buyers are satisfied with a product, the company should attempt to find out why the remaining 5% are not, so that it can make improvements in quality.

Strategic, or Environmental Scanning

Strategic, or environmental scanning combines all the remaining forms of scanning. The task is to conduct careful monitoring of the economic, social, political, ecological, and legal environment in which the company operates.

What information should be gathered on the environment?

With strategic scanning, you set out to detect the possible sources of crisis that might affect the company's operations, then, once they have been identified, to define the means to be implemented in response.

Obviously, no strategy is entirely immune to political risks that can destabilize the company. The information system should therefore enable the company to accomplish the following.

• To identify possible sources of political risk that might affect the countries in which it operates and the way they treat foreign companies established there. Consulting firms have worked out systems that classify nations according to how risky it is to invest there. The risks involved are then evaluated with the help of "warning lights" that correspond to the benchmarks worked out for each country. The scenario method combines socioeconomic simulation with industrial analysis of the relevant countries. Yet the approach that we consider most interesting and that fits in best with the notion of scanning is the rarer method of dynamic segmentation, which consists of observing social, political, and demographic disparities capable of generating conflict, then of mapping out the possible alliances or antagonisms between these different segments.[1]

• To assess the possible impact of such problems on the company's overseas operations and on its holdings in the countries involved.

A brief list of possible sources of political risk might include the following:

– The strategic importance of the industry or line of business involved for the host country.

– The attitude of the company's home country toward the host country's government and institutions (leaders, political parties, trade unions, etc.).

– The nationality of the company setting up operations in the host country.

– Social conflict in the host country.

– Measures adopted by the host country in the sphere of politics, economics, and individual freedom.

If we look at the problem in greater detail, we can distinguish four major sub-categories of strategic scanning. A few examples should help to clarify them.

---

1. *Ibid.*

Geopolitical Scanning

Geopolitical scanning involves keeping a close watch on the balance of power emerging, for example, out of the ruins of the Eastern bloc, in the context of larger, regional alliances. In order to carry out this kind of scanning properly, we need to attend major events like the Davos Forum, conferences held by L'Expansion, the World Future Society, etc., and to work regularly with various organizations and think-tanks concerned with the future.

Geographical Scanning

What kind of preparations should we make for setting up business in the two mega-markets of the year 2000, i.e. China and India, and how can we achieve deep-going alliances with peoples whose culture is so remote from ours?

Legal and Legislative Scanning

What new legal frameworks will emerge from the process of European unification, and what implications will they have for your industry? Answering this question requires keeping up on raw materials and processes used around the world.

Societal Scanning

Among the shifts in behavior that can currently be observed, some will have decisive influence on many companies' choice of business and strategy.

• **The position women will hold in society in the year 2000.** Serious thought should be devoted to the role of women in the economy and the rise of culturally "feminine" values in our socioeconomic structures, in order to develop appropriate responses.

• **The behavior patterns of young people.** In the fall of 1996, the French women's magazine *Elle* published an in-depth survey of "the Kleenex generation," i.e. today's 20-year-olds. The magazine describes how young people resort to networking, mutual aid, and plain ingenuity, without really believing in the promises held out by their political and economic environment.

• **The effect of the "greying" of the population on markets.** It has become essential to take the elderly, their needs, and their opinions into account. Any careful observer now knows that a gradual shift is taking place in advertising, as TV commercials for the Volkswagen Sharan or for Nivea skin cream clearly show.

• **The direction in which the concept of luxury is heading and the way in which our society perceives it.** The concept of luxury has less and less to do with the codes traditionally associated with it (e.g.

conspicuous consumption, unaffordable goods). Today's consumers seem to have something else in mind, a kind of intangible, immaterial luxury composed of leisure time, travel, and unique experiences.

• **The influence of multimedia on buying patterns.** Swatch has set up an Internet game site called Cyber Swatch for presenting its products, which has broken visitors' records. The watchmaking firm has thereby developed a "fun" image associated with change and modernity. Large companies like the mail-order firm La Redoute have started selling their products on the Web, while others such as Estée Lauder are seriously contemplating a similar move.

The Tools of Scanning

Competitive Benchmarking

As everyone knows, benchmarking means comparing a company's results in a given area (logistics, order processing, etc.) with the results achieved by the firm considered the best in that area. This practice is especially useful in competitive scanning to the extent that it forces you to decide what really counts for your company. You should first determine which activities are in need of improvement, then measure performance in those areas against the "best of class."

It is obviously hard to find direct competitors who willingly collaborate and disclose their company secrets. For that reason, it often proves to be more enlightening to observe the methods used in other industries than to confine yourself to familiar ground. Even practices that are quite different from the ones used in your industry can provide you with useful analyses and guidelines. This is where case studies come in. The scanning unit at L'Oréal audited a number of companies that were totally unrelated to its line of work (e.g. the FNAC book and record store, Moulinex, Lefranc-Bourgeois, Sony, Walmart, home catering operations, and florists) in order to figure out what shifts had occurred in terms of distribution systems and channels.

On-the-spot Reporting

Writing up this kind of report could become a virtually automatic reaction after every trade show, factory visit, or trip abroad. Some departments could create targeted newsletters so as to make sure that the information gathered in this way gets distributed to the right people, rather than going to waste.

The "Datawarehouse"

The "datawarehouse" enables a company to base its decisions on a global vision of all data manipulated in the course of operations. This system, which is becoming more and more widespread, can make a significant contribution to scanning activities.

In highly competitive industries, this tool may be used to improve logistics or marketing techniques. Several supermarket chains, for example, have set up gigantic datawarehouses in order to monitor in real time what is happening on its shelves and to strengthen the loyalty of today's increasingly fickle consumer. In every industry, thorough knowledge on customers has become a key asset for maximizing the income they generate. What makes this new technique particularly interesting is that according to recent studies, it yields a rather quick return on investment, i.e. in only three years' time.

In addition to datawarehouses, there now exists what is known as "datamining," which involves digging up data through cross-referencing in order to prevent information from "killing off" information. Any number of such systems have been developed, which give priority to selecting, storing, and analyzing information available on Internet by surfing from site to site.

> *Knowing how to distribute information is also*
> *essential to scanning.*

Work on the flow of information is essential, and should be regarded as a full-fledged tool. We have to circulate information that reflects the company's priorities. In this area as well, we need to move from the logic of managing stock–to which we are all accustomed–to the logic of managing flow, so we can optimize efficiency and keep scanning activities from producing an information overdose.

Yet we always come up against the same obstacles. At a certain point, a weak signal tends to cause trouble, because it usually represents a deviation from the conformist standpoint. Thus, when a deviant signal is picked up, it tends to be either minimized or overtly rejected. The skill that those practicing competitive intelligence need to master is to be able to induce other company members to take hold of the weak signals that have been detected and to exploit whatever potential benefit their development may hold.

As Albert Jacquard so rightly put it, "Information means shaping; communication means sharing."

In laboratory work, for example, scanning agents must know how to stimulate research people, to mobilize them, to impress upon them the issues involved, to turn scanning into an act of collaboration. As we mentioned earlier, this is precisely what 3M does, by organizing an annual function so that technical staff from company branches around the world can exchange their ideas.

Needless to say, this task has to be accomplished in a credible way. One scanning representative for a whole lab full of research people is clearly an unrealistic ratio.

The Importance of Networking

Any activity aimed at monitoring the environment should be understood as the product of a network of information providers.

There are a number of good opportunities and institutions for this purpose, including the Club de l'Expansion forums, the Davos Forum, or the many think-tanks like the World Future Society that have burgeoned in The United States, Germany, and Japan. Companies can use such sources and occasions to garner key information for decision-making.

Having scanning personnel take part in the leading think-tanks can help to make other company members more aware of issues that the firm as a whole does not necessarily emphasize.

In addition to such structures, networks of informants can be developed and maintained. Acting as the company's "antennae," such informants may be experts or people who are continually in touch with practical reality out in the field. After careful observation, they can express their opinions either in ad hoc meetings, by teleconference, by e-mail, or other electronic means.

It is crucial today to know how to take advantage of these networks on a world scale, so that people from Japan, Singapore, the United States, South America, and Europe can conduct an ongoing dialogue.

EXAMPLE
_____

■ MEMBERS OF THE WELL NETWORK, set up by the Global Business Network, can freely bring up a subject, with anyone else allowed to contribute to the discussion. Scanning lookouts must be able to join all such networks in order to gather information that goes beyond the mere microeconomic framework.

_____

The Lookout's Profile

In this respect, the lookout's profile is an essential factor in determining how effective scanning activity will be. The lookout must be someone who is good at networking and establishing new ties, someone who enjoys recognition from both superiors and research workers. The scanning unit should not be viewed as a design department, a statistics bureau, or a modeling team.

It may therefore be important to create a set of stimuli to increase recognition for the scanning unit or to develop a sense of belonging, to give greater legitimacy to scanning staff in relation to other company members and the hierarchy. There are all kinds of possibilities that have yet to be explored.

"Whoever monitors weak signals must first make them visible and extract them from the surrounding noise, in order to benefit from the intelligence on the future that such signals often carry."

In his book *Competitive Intelligence*,[1] Larry Kahaner asserts that the person in charge of economic intelligence in a company should play the role of "the King's jester". George Charpak uses a similar metaphor to characterize relations between scientists and their government, one that may safely be extended to scanning lookouts as well.

To conclude, we will present a few recommendations for anyone who plans to engage in scanning. Here are the basic requirements.

1. Steer clear of the dangers inherent in any scanning system and maintain the quality of information. The main pitfalls here are gradual burn-out, false information, the inability to perceive new phenomena, the excessively narrow horizons of some consulting firms (particularly those that have neither international scope nor global vision).

2. Create awareness and motivation among all other company members as to the importance of constantly gathering fresh information. The company should send people out to seminars and on study trips in search of information, and then make sure to update it continually. Such work should be a part of everyone's job description.

3. Avoid associating exclusively with specialists. Scanning is everybody's business. Above all, it requires a general frame of mind based on curiosity, openmindedness, and rigorous thinking.

4. Maintain a state of creative tension. Watchfulness and action are two complementary sides of a company's intelligence. Scanning requires a healthy restlessness, a constant state of alert.

We are living in an increasingly immaterial economy. Feelings and qualitative factors are steadily gaining ground over rationality and quantitative factors. Likewise, the development of one-to-one relations with customers is taking us far afield from the economies of scale that were the hallmark of the mass production era.

In the future, business success will depend on the ability to tap the energy and intelligence of everyone in the company. An open, attentive attitude toward what people say and want is highly conducive to innovation, risk-taking, and the acquiring of new knowledge. In the service sector in particular, excellence and competitive advantage can only be achieved by mobilizing employees' energy and regularly expanding their skill base. But even in more traditional businesses, goods and services now include large quantities of brain power, because producing them requires the input of several different disciplines. Every product or service results from a complex body of information, especially since consumer behavior patterns have become harder to pinpoint.

---

1. Larry Kahaner, *Competitive Intelligence* (Simon and Schuster, 1996).

Today's consumer is a mutlifaceted, chameleon-like creature. This is yet another reason why everyone in the company should be sticking his or her head outside, in order to catch a whiff of what is really going on.

THE NEED FOR A KEEN SENSE OF SMELL

7

Consumers now have the power to make or break an innovation. Their response to a new offer is as binding as the law.

In the postwar boom period, companies were often confronted with a demand that outstripped possible supply. The converse is true today. Furthermore, customers now evince an increasingly demanding, critical attitude when it comes to having their individual needs met.

The consumer's life project is our business.

To treat self-fulfillment and the development of human knowledge as key values is to deal with the notion of life project. This also holds true for the industrial world. A learning organization–especially one that produces consumer goods–has to get back in touch with its ultimate reference point, the consumer, and take an active interest in his or her life project.

This situation results from a new demand for service quality. After shifting from a society based on mass production to one in which the distributor was king, we now appear to be entering an era in which the customer holds the essential power. In spite of the dizzying variety of goods and services now on the market, the consumer often shows considerable frustration, claiming that no one is providing what he or she really wants.

Whereas in the 1980s, consumers faced a "take it or leave it" situation, they are now the ones who are dictating terms, selecting those companies that are willing and able to "deliver the goods." Giving consumers greater satisfaction and making life easier for them must be the goal of any firm that wants to stay competitive.

As a result, we have to engage in continual auditing of consumer desires and satisfaction levels, using surveys that provide detailed information on both "hard" and "soft" features. The product-service couple is no longer optional; it has become a necessary component of any corporate strategy. What still remains to be accomplished, however, is to place even greater emphasis on the emotional satisfaction that consumers derive from the purchase act itself.

EXAMPLE

■ THE IMAGE OF HERMÈS is so laden with intangibles that buying a Hermès product offers a certain emotional satisfaction–despite the seemingly prohibitive cost of so many of the firm's items.

Admittedly, consumer attitudes will not be easy to audit, and the problem is compounded by the flood of data with which new information technology constantly swamps us.

Be that as it may, the new technology has other implications as well. It has brought about the emergence of a new kind of consumer: the cyber-consumer. "According to a survey conducted by the Credoc towards the end of 1996, 35% of all French people believe that in the coming years, they will be in a position to accomplish more things at home with new computer technology... The desire for home consumption is at the top of the list when consumers are asked what they imagine that multimedia will enable them to do more often... The prospect of home shopping goes hand in hand with the desire for more communication or easier access to all sorts of information, both national and international. Network computing would then enter into competition with traditional media by offering previously undreamt possibilities for interaction." [1]

These developments should encourage us to think about new behavior patterns that are likely to shake up all our strategies. Our whole concept of promotion and advertising needs to be revised and tailored to a more sedentary consumer, with the emphasis being placed on sidestepping traditional distribution channels.

In the future, decisions will be made on the basis of factual, immediately available information, rather than at the manufacturer's initiative. A revolution in advertising is clearly in the offing. The key task today is to "relearn" from consumers, to take all their new temptations into account. There already exist Internet forums and bold new initia-

---

1. Patrick Babayou, "Vers le cyberconsommateur," *in* Credoc, *Consommation et modes de vie*, March 1997.

tives like the one launched by CFDP, a small insurance company that involves its customers in working out the appropriate insurance products.

The economy is losing its material substance,
while requiring ever greater amounts of
service.

Technological progress has generated a powerful "dematerialization" of the economy. Expenditures on information technology, on R & D, on training and education, on marketing, on organization and management are all shifting strategic resources away from material goods to immaterial goods. This is not simply a question of the decline of the industrial sector in relation to the service sector. More interestingly, it has to do with the introduction of a service component into the processes of industrial production itself. What this really boils down to is that service has become predominant in the creation of value.

Before being compelled to submit to brutal restructuring, companies should endeavor to grasp these different factors, while reconceiving the way in which they are organized. Thus, the principle of reengineering revolves around four points.

• Determining which processes take priority.
• Rethinking the whole company in terms of these key processes (possibly with the assistance of customers).
• Adopting an integrated strategic, operational, systemic approach.
• Marking a sharp break with existing practice and reshaping processes with the help of everyone involved.

The Easy Way Out: Formalization

Rigid Resistance to Change

As we pointed out earlier, companies that have reached a certain size and importance often suffer from bureaucracy and sluggish complacency.

All institutions are in danger of falling into internal entropy and "the dinosaur syndrome," characterized by overly centralized bureaucracy. When they do, it takes a growing mass of rules, paperwork, and special authorizations to handle even the most routine questions. Any decision requires endless meetings. Problems are regularly shunted from department to department. Managers are less and less willing to take the slightest risk, internal communications are poor, and the decision-making process drags on and on, with a corresponding decline in capacity for rapid response. The sense of efficiency that perhaps prevailed when the organization was still fairly flexible gets weaker all the time.[1]

When companies suffering from such bureaucratic inertia fall upon hard times, they tend to react by tightening controls even further, thus increasing the already high level of stress. The end result is to reinforce inertia. Bogged down in office politics, the firms concentrate mainly on solving internal contradictions. This self-absorbed attitude gradually leads them to lose any sense of their outside environment, much to the delight of their competitors.

EXAMPLE

■ AT ONE OF THE WORLD'S LEADING COMPANIES IN THE FIELD OF WATER PURIFICATION, focus on internal problems intensified to such an extent that customers, i.e. the people who represented demand for the firm's services, came to be seen as a source of disturbance. The company was finally bought out.

This syndrome of "self-absorbed inertia" develops along with growth. More than ever before, today's large corporations need to use methods that stimulate initiative, innovation, and creativity.

How can bureacratization be avoided?

There are a number of ways to avoid the tendency toward bureaucracy in any organization, many of which are surprisingly simple.
- Examine the validity of all paperwork.
- Break approval procedures down into clear-cut stages.
- Get the right people involved in a project as soon as it starts.
- Test a variety of approaches quickly.
- Hunt down all technical bottlenecks.
- Give ample preparation to the person to whom a project is to be submitted.
- Set aside enough time for hashing out points of agreement and disagreement.

When it comes to circulating, developing, using, or appropriating knowledge, the key concept turns out to be *process*.

---

1. *Cf.* Robert Salmon, *The Future of Management* (Blackwell, 1996), reporting remarks by Kasuma Dateichi.

EXAMPLE

■ BY FOLLOWING A STEP-BY-STEP RATIONAL APPROACH, the Americans succeeded in sending 500,000 men to Kuwait and deploying a vast logistical support system that enabled them to reconquer the country.

Controlling processes does not always require formalizing them.

Let's consider a few examples of formalized processes that are nonetheless inadequately controlled.

• Repeated promotional campaigns to boost sales artificially can do damage to brand image.

• Selling excessively large volumes of a newly introduced product may create a problem of overstocking for retailers, who will then be reluctant to reorder.

• Constant meetings held purportedly to solve problems often mask a lack of pragmatic thinking.

This is by no means a minor issue. Managers spend far too much time in meetings. As a result of hierarchical structures (or rather, bureaucratic ones), companies find themselves obligated to organize meetings involving a wide variety of people, at least half of whom are in no position to solve the problems discussed. In truly successful companies, which usually emphasize networking rather than bureaucracy, a number of experts carefully examine all projects, and they are the only ones whose presence is required at the relevant meetings. The CEO of Toyota claims he never goes to meetings, because "otherwise, no one else speaks up."

In "Latin" countries like France and Italy, there is little concern for process. Of course, scrupulously applying the rules can stifle imagination, but there are some aspects of process that must be upheld if we want to generate effective discussion and unleash the creative energy of all company members.

EXAMPLE

■ IN MEETINGS HELD IN THE UNITED STATES, the functions of facilitator and observer have practically become institutionalized. At Stanford University, for example, one person is put in charge of overseeing the way in which discussions are conducted, paying more attention to process than to content.

In France, where we hold regular meetings, it would be advisable to adopt a few basic principles designed to improve process.
    – Keep away disruptive elements who have little to contribute.
    – Establish clear objectives and a shared vision.
    – Clarify procedures for implementing decisions.
    – Fix stimulating, but realistic deadlines.
    • Comparison of different cultures reveals, for example, that the Japanese notion of what constitutes creativity is totally unlike the Latin vision.[1]
    • In Latin countries, people tend to assume that either you're a genius or you aren't (although genius is usually short-lived and doomed to decline some day).
    • The Japanese believe you can master the processes that make it possible to acquire knowledge and add value. This is a less chancy, more solid approach.
    To avoid squandering knowledge and to mobilize their people, then, companies should do away with poorly structured meetings, ill-defined objectives, muddled discussions, and insufficiently prepared decision-making. We must also simplify language, keeping in-group lingo and professional jargon down to a minimum.

Getting Closer to the Customer Through Customization

    In traditional marketing, new ideas gave rise to market research, followed by product development, testing, and finally rollout. In contrast, the current context compels firms to engage in marketing based on thorough familiarity with all the components of their line of business.

The Development of Soft Science

    Contemporary marketing methods, which make increasingly sophisticated use of new technology, focus much more on consumer behavior patterns. Every transaction is now viewed as a piece of information that can be capitalized on and turned into profit.
    Consumers pay for each purchase twice, the first time with money, and the second time by providing information on their buying behav-

---

1. For a serious analysis of such comparisons, see Charles Hampden-Turner and Alfons Trompenaars, *The Seven Cultures of Capitalism* (Doubleday, New York, 1993). In our Appendix, we present their statistical findings regarding responses to important dilemmas faced by corporate leaders from different cultures.

ior, i.e. on their relationship to the product, to the company that manufactures it, and to the retailer who sells it. As we saw in the last chapter, such information can be stored in a powerful data base (or "datawarehouse"), then related to other information by equally powerful tools ("datamining"), and finally transformed into a new product –also marketable–that might be referred to as a "knowledge product."

Thus, classical marketing, which consists mainly of vaunting the efficiency of a product, is now enhanced through a new approach that we shall call *marketing through capitalizing on the information contained in consumer purchase acts.*

*New information technology opens the way to a
new kind of marketing.*

Three new marketing techniques are currently being applied.

1. *Micro-marketing* segments consumer populations into behavior categories according to a number of previously defined criteria (e.g. age, income, geographic location, and shopping location).

2. *Guerrilla marketing*, as the name indicates, takes advantage of special events that bring crowds together (sports events, cultural festivals, etc.) to target potential customers.

3. *Frequency marketing* seeks above all to reward customer loyalty, which also serves to raise the quality of information received on the buying patterns of regular customers.

These new forms of marketing aim not only at getting through to the final customer and winning his or her loyalty, but also at capitalizing on the data collected in this fashion in order to magnify the power of the company's information systems. Such a strategy has become a matter of life and death.

To avoid a situation in which you have a wealth of data but a paucity of real information, you must simultaneously work on the following points.

1. Identify key data on targeted customers.

2. Transform this raw data into usable information.

3. Employ statistical methods to analyse and anticipate consumer behavior.

4. Assess the findings.

5. React to the opportunities that emerge from this assessment so as to create a set of personalized relations with consumers.

As regards micro-marketing, however, it should be stressed that consumer profiles are no longer as differentiated as they were a few years ago. This shift is particularly noteworthy in the area of women's magazines, as the information needs of students merge increasingly with those of working women.

The question of trust will soon dominate
relations with consumers.

Traditional marketing revolved around simultaneous efforts to gain market share and to achieve economies of scale. Over the past several years, however, the mass market has broken up into a myriad of smaller markets, each one characterized by distinct needs and behavior patterns. It is becoming increasingly important to stop treating the consumer as one element in a vast, homogeneous set and to start viewing him or her as a unique individual representing an authentic economic unit.

A shift in perspective is clearly required. Instead of merely promoting transactions, we have to establish relations. The new goal of marketing is to offer value to the right customer at the right time. Mutual trust, which has assumed vital importance in relations between members of any given profession, will also come to dominate the relationship between manufacturer or retailer and final customer.

One-to-one Marketing

Both an art and a science, one-to-one marketing proves to be much more complex than traditional, transaction-based marketing. Any firm that wishes to practice it needs to possess the following assets.

• Detailed information on customers as well as high-powered data bases.

• Sophisticated techniques for evaluating customers and market segments.

• Ultra-precise methods for targeting resources and advertising messages, for managing networks or channels, and for analyzing the findings.

Companies that have mastered these tools get the competitive edge. Thus, the French mega-store chain Carrefour, which, up until a few years ago, was far behind its formidable rival Walmart in terms of new information technology, has given top priority to mastery of this technology. Owing to this dogged determination on the part of top management, Carrefour has succeeded in overcoming its initial handicap.

As messages and media become increasingly
fragmented, conventional marketing tools lose
much of their former efficiency.

"Marketing has become a serious handicap for consumer goods producers," stated a recent article in *The Economist.* Employing many of the usual tools–advertising in the leading news media, cash vouchers, point-of-sale promotions–is a little bit like using a cannon to shoot birds. The more messages and media become fragmented, the less effective such methods are.

The same cannot be said of one-to-one marketing, which collects detailed information on every customer. It enables firms to tailor their messages and campaigns to the specific incentives appropriate to each consumer or market segment. This results in higher marketing productivity and therefore a better return on investment. The most agile companies in this area get excellent results and a distinct competitive advantage over competitors.

Five essential factors distinguish any true one-to-one marketing strategy.

1. Lasting relations with the customer. Each transaction is put in the broader perspective of the overall relationship between the firm and the customer. Thus, campaigns or other forms of communication may be motivated by nothing other than the need to build relationships. Rather than seeking short-term sales, the aim is to take the customer's long-term perceptions and behavior patterns into account.

2. Two-way communication flows. One-to-one marketing means endeavoring to start or to maintain an ongoing dialogue with the customer.

EXAMPLE

■ **PETER ARTZT, PROCTER & GAMBLE'S CHIEF EXECUTIVE,** stresses that by using interactive communication, companies will gain greater influence over both technological change and behavior patterns in our society. "We have always shaped the communication environment so that it meets our needs. It is now up to us to take hold of the electronic networks and to force Internet to work in our interest. We can use interactivity to have the consumer participate in our advertising. We can get immediate response. If we do a good job, people will be riveted to their chairs in front of their computers when the ads appear."

---

3. Economies of scope rather than scale. In one-to-one marketing, the goal is to deepen the relationship with each customer, rather than to increase the number of customers.

4. Adaptive strategies. To maintain long-term relationships, companies must follow–or even anticipate–the desires of the customers targeted by tirelessly refining its offer so as to pull ahead of the pack.

5. A concern for marketing productivity. Adaptive strategies must be based on systems for evaluation and follow-up that make it possible to determine the efficiency of each marketing initiative and to monitor the leading indicators of the company's competitive position.

One-to-one marketing isn't Chinese–or is it?

Oddly enough, the real masters of the art of one-to-one marketing seem to be the Chinese. Their line of reasoning is that once you develop a relationship, the transaction will follow, owing to a combination of the five "F"s: family, friend, fast, flexible, fun. In contrast, Westerners, who are steeped in transactional marketing, count more on the five "P"s: price, product, promotion, place, and performance. As a result, they tend to focus on single transactions, imagining that relationships will flow automatically from them. To our way of thinking, the Chinese are closer to the truth. You're better off making relationships the number one concern and considering everything else in terms of this focus.

Yet however important it is to create long-term relationships with customers, the first step in this direction is obviously constant quality improvement.

From Intuition to Innovation

The Many Facets of Quality

Quality is indissociable from the notion of process. In the field of quality management, it has been discovered that 15% of all flaws can be attributed to human agents, with the remaining 85% due to the way the system is organized. This observation unquestionably has serious implications for the analysis of processes.

The activity of most companies can be broken down into a number of distinct processes. What distinguishes one firm from another is the number of processes it makes use of–and their quality. For example, a typical operational process involves product development, the winning over of new customers, identification of customers' needs, production, logistic support, purchasing management, and customer service.

The interesting question is which function, or stage in the process, the company chooses to stress.

Perceptions regarding this problem vary considerably from one region of the industrialized world to another.

• In the United States, the idea is to produce high-quality goods at a reasonable price.

• In Europe, the emphasis is placed on adapting to a changing market.

• In Japan, the chief concern is to turn out a steady stream of new, almost custom-made products for customers.

The Americans and the Japanese have found a way to apply the principle of reengineering to their processes so as to improve quality and gain greater control over time. But this brand of reengineering must always be practiced in a broad, general framework.

Getting to Market Fast

The remarkable competitive edge that comes from getting to market fast is clearly illustrated by the race between Honda and Yamaha.

EXAMPLE

■ **When Honda began to move into foreign markets, Yamaha** attempted to take advantage of the situation to attack its rival by bringing out 37 models in a single year. Honda, however, responded by flooding the market, producing 113 models in just 18 months. Thus, in record time, Honda succeeded in crushing Yamaha under this avalanche of new products. This example demonstrates that control of time frames can be a lethal weapon.

In today's economy, marked by the rapid spread of information technology, speed will play an increasingly important role. MacKinsey estimates that a 6-month lag in developing a product translates into a 36% drop in profits, whereas fixing sales costs 9% higher than they might be causes a decline of only 22%. In contrast, overspending by 50% in development costs brings about a loss of no more than 3.5%.

The notion of product life cycle is crucial in this regard. The powerful surge of Japanese car sales dates back to the time at which the Japanese automakers figured out how to reduce the design-to-market cycle to less than 3 years, while it still took their Western competitors between 5 and 7 years (although the latter have more or less caught up since then). Companies that know how to put product life cycle to good use can gain a formidable competitive advantage.

Flexibility

By emphasizing flexibility, we do little more than to take our lead from an increasingly demanding consumer. Company flexibility constitutes a response to a recently felt need, since consumers now want more custom-made products, including products they help to design —provided it can be done at no extra cost.

■ SWATCH provides a perfect illustration of this trend, giving consumers the impression that when they choose a particular Swatch model, they are buying the design that suits them best.

Kokubu, a Japanese custom-built bicycle manufacturer, offers an astounding selection of 11,231,862 possible made-to-order combinations, with a 10-day delivery time and a price that is only 10% higher than for standard models.

The shift toward flexibility reflects the new need to produce a large number of items in smaller batches. This idea is admirably summed up by Nissan's slogan of the five "anys": anything, in any volume, at any time, for any budget.

Variety

We have entered the era of "mass customization," a trend affecting a wide range of goods and services, from books, cassettes, and sewing machines to personalized insurance policies.

■ ALTHOUGH AIR CONDITIONING IN CARS used to be seen as a luxury item, it now belongs to standard equipment in many models. "Having air conditioning is no longer a plus; not having it is a minus."

Innovation and Creativity

The obligation to innovate means not only creating new products, but also developing the creativity of company members and, to this end, updating management methods. In this area, Europe lags behind the United States, since the vital importance of innovation and creativity has yet to register fully on European managers.

Innovation is a decisive factor in keeping a company moving–and ahead of the pack. The questions we should be asking are: What are the processes involved in creativity? What practices make it easier to manage creative projects?

In some industries, the speed of strategic cycles can be turned to account for creative purposes. (What we mean by strategic cycles is a series of phases in which the prevailing ideas are challenged by the advent of a new cycle.) The new *strategic cycle* starts at the same time as a new Sigmoid curve (*cf.* Ch. 1).

Sometimes, new possibilities appear early on to innovators and precursors before they are widely recognized as such. Most observers underestimated the impact of any number of breakthroughs (the fax, the Minitel, E-mail, Internet). To build the future, we have to free ourselves from the short-sightedness that makes us prisoners of existing markets. One of the tasks of competitive intelligence is to monitor the weak signals heralding innovations that may otherwise be hard to predict.

As regard the way they relate to innovation, companies may be divided up into five groups.

- The innovators.
- The forerunners.
- The early majority.
- The late majority.
- The stragglers.

Businesses that continue to innovate at a sustained pace usually manage to grow faster than the others. They stay in the lead as long as they consider innovation a vital process, one that is neither too costly nor too chancy, compared to the risk involved in falling behind or getting wiped out. It cannot be sufficiently stressed that the greatest risk has become not taking any risks at all.

Furthermore, in today's context of technological upheaval, only full assimilation of the data provided by competitive intelligence makes it possible to innovate. Innovation cannot be treated in isolation from reality. It has to meet people's expectations half-way. In the last analysis, of course, pure innovation may be able to create future consumer needs. The manufacturer who innovates proposes, but it is the non-innovative consumer who disposes. It is he or she who enjoys the inordinate privilege of making or breaking an offer.

> *Continual innovation should be encouraged as much as quantum leaps in technology.*

Creativity and innovation are all too often reduced to the idea of generating something out of nothing. To a considerable extent, however, innovation now also involves improving upon concepts or simplifying existing products in order to render them more effective.

Innovation should be every company member's business. Even fundamental breakthroughs require the support and participation of the entire organization in order to come to fruition. As for quantum leaps in technology, they too need to be followed through with a mass of incremental improvements.

By mobilizing energy throughout the firm, by empowering people to come up with ideas and to implement them, we move from a management style based on procedure and control to one that encourages people to express their creativity. We must build organisations that give everyone a chance to innovate. It is particularly important to discourage marketing managers from seeking the comfort of life at corporate headquarters. They should be out there in the field, hunting around for new creative resources.

To stimulate innovation, we have to abandon our traditional linear, rationalistic way of thinking and give our imaginations free rein to establish connections between seemingly unrelated things.

EXAMPLE

- IT WAS THE COMBINATION OF PLASTIC TECHNOLOGY with microchip technology that enabled Moreno to invent the smart card. It was the study of dolphins' skin that paved the way for improvements in diving suits. And it was analysis of how thistles cling to the corduroys of hikers in the woods that led to the invention of Velcro.

From Information to Knowledge

Thus, a growing concern for the processes behind quality and innovation (both technical and commercial) is what makes it possible to gain and to maintain the competitive edge. Success therefore depends on the behavior, the spirit of initiative, and the imagination of all company members, whatever their position may be.

This explains why some many of today's companies are focusing heavily on the human factor, on people and their values, while seeking to strike a more harmonious balance between business efficiency and individual fulfillment.

Creating a Learning Organization

Information, work, and education are thus destined to merge increasingly. People demonstrate their professionalism today by expanding their horizons, which entails not only the obvious solution of going back to school, but also turning every job experience into an opportunity to learn and grow.

Truly successful companies never cease to acquire new knowledge. Yet this ability to transform experience into knowledge is much less common among more ordinary firms. To facilitate learning, it is advisable to set up multidisciplinary teams based on project rather than on function. We should also devote thought and formal study to a phenomenon that turns out to be more complex than it looks: learning. It may well be that we need to "learn how to learn".[1]

LEARNING TO LEARN

People learn in a cyclical fashion, shifting constantly back and forth between thought and action. Like predatory animals, they silently and calmly lie in wait, accumulating information and connecting it. When they decide to act, they pounce. Whether they succeed or fail, they return to the waiting stage, enriched, however, by this additional experience, which raises their level of knowledge.

This series of phases is not limited to hunters. Lovers, researchers, and artists also go through the following cycle.

1. Reflecting (perception).

2. Connecting (an aptitude more highly developed in human beings than in other animals).

3. Deciding.

4. Doing.

This cycle then immediately becomes the object of further reflection.

1. **Reflecting** is becoming observers of our own thinking and acting (as well as of the thinking and acting of the world around us). Did the event correspond to pre-established mental models, or should a new schema be developed to take both distant experiences and the most recent experience into account? We are constantly compelled to choose between competing schemas.

We don't always need repeated experiences to constitute an image of the outside world. Sometimes, powerful single experiences are enough (e.g. to kill our taste for a particular food). In terms of perception, we even have an easier time recalling new, mobile phenomena than constant or repetitive ones.

Memory is a process rather than a place. It is not static; it shuttles back and forth between concept and reality as a way to reduce the complexity of this reality. The natural reflex that enables us to achieve this is known as "chunking." We subdivide a problem by grouping bits of information together (in "chunks") in order to be able

---

1. The following passage represents a synthesis of conversations held with Brad Hoyt in March 1997.

to recall them. Memory is the result of this process rather than a system for filing raw data.

Two forms of memory can thus be distinguished. In *episodic memory*, we record a reflection as a series of events, almost like a movie camera. In contrast, *reflective memory* uses concepts and schemas that both structure and modify what is perceived. It would be a mistake, however, to assume that episodic memory is the more accurate of the two forms. There is nothing trickier than reconstituting a precise chronological order, even in the case of "flashbulb memory events" like the Kennedy assassination. Memory often scrambles the sequence of events, and tests have shown that we should above all be wary of memories about events which we are convinced we recall accurately. They are the ones that usually contain the highest number of errors.

Our reflective modes can also be inaccurate, as a result of mental habits and the lazy refusal to question a pre-existing schema. For example, the human body *seems* to have two halves, each the mirror image of the other. In fact, however, anatomical, functional, or neurological observation already contradicted this supposed symmetry, which reflects the categories of human thought much more than reality itself. Thus, biological reference books used to proclaim that human cells had genes arranged on 24 pairs of chromosomes, even though it was widely known that there were 23. Scientists take note of such a discovery, but fail to consider the implications. And when one of these fictions is finally unmasked, you usually find that the people in the field will say with some impatience: "Yes, of course. Everyone knows that!"

Information is thus subject to the dictates of reflection. We force reality to fit in with a degree of certainty or a definite character that it doesn't actually possess. When we fail to perceive signals correctly because we are functioning on the basis of an erroneous schema, we are likely to be heading for a crisis.

2. **Connecting** involves reducing information to models, or sometimes, in a burst of creativity, inventing a new schema. Connection consists of seeing what we have always seen and thinking what we have never thought. Archimedes, Newton, Darwin, and Einstein hit upon their theories in a "flash of genius." This is the phenomenon of *the inductive leap*. Everything falls into place, irrelevancies relate, and dissonance becomes harmony. The important thing is not so much to obtain new facts, but to discover new ways of thinking about them.

Our brain constantly seeks connections. In dreams, in particular, it constructs scenarios, most of them sheer nonsense and discarded the moment we wake. Our notion of reality, as we perceive it, depends on what it is filtered through. In fact, the past is often reconstructed as we learn more about it. This is why historical events seem clearer several centuries later than a few years after they occur.

Talking to ourselves is part of our connective consciousness. Our lives are intertwined with narrative, with the stories we tell and hear. We constantly recount and reassess the meaning of past actions, while anticipating the outcome of future projects. It is our ability to choose between such alternative scenarios that constitutes our free will. But our choices are only as good as our imagination in constructing a wide range of candidate scenarios.

Premature closure in connection occurs in children, probably because of their short attention span. But in adults, it may be their logical framework. When something fits, it is accepted and we stop looking for alternatives. As Nietzsche noted, "Convictions are more dangerous enemies of truth than lies."

Conviction, like those two other major poles of distraction, pain and pleasure, brings the connecting phase to an end. According to Minsky, "We can program a computer to solve any problem by trial and error, without knowing how to solve it in advance, provided only that we have a way to recognize when the problem is solved." For human beings, unlike computers, have emotions. And they are essential to the next phase after connecting: deciding.

3. **Deciding** is settling on a method of action. Although everyone knows that too much emotion wreaks havoc on decision-making, what is less known is that essentially emotionally impaired people lack basic rational decision-making abilities. After decades of artificial intelligence work, MIT researchers have concluded that unemotional, rule-based computers remain unable to think and make decisions.

This emotional content is also vital to effective communication of decisions. If the decision-maker's affect does not make the meaning of his or her decision explicit, people tend to fill it in, and often wrongly.

4. **Doing,** the last of our four phases, is what determines whether the whole process succeeds or fails. Some parts of our minds learn mainly from success, which tends to aim and focus how we think. But other parts of our minds learn mainly by mistakes, by remembering the circumstances in which various methods failed to work, although this may be less gratifying. Paradoxically, however, it turns out that learning from positive experience rarely leads to major improvements in what we already do. It sometimes even seems that failure is a prerequisite to progress in knowledge.

This line of thinking helps to explain why the high hopes initially placed in artificial intelligence have been scaled back. Information technology has no real access to the meaning of words, since computers are devoid of emotion. Only human beings can understand the nature, the import, and the consequences of their acts. This means that the new information technology cannot be viewed as an end in itself, but at most as a vehicle for getting around in the world of knowledge.

> *We have abandoned the mechanistic vision of*
> *man as machine.*

The predominant vision of the world towards the beginning of the twentieth century stemmed from a paradigm based on the primacy of technique over human labor. Artificial intelligence appeared to be the logical extension of this paradigm, offering the hope that technical progress could equal the achievements of the human brain.

The human being was supposed to function as much as possible according to machine reflex, in a system based on the division of a labor and the standardization of all tasks. The fact of the matter is, however, that people are endowed with knowledge and are therefore capable of transcending a given system. As a result, the mechanistic vision has fallen apart.

> *Human knowledge is the crucial asset of the*
> *future.*

It is becoming increasingly clear that the main determinant of excellence and competitive strength is the human, organizational factor. This is why it is so important to kindle and to nurture the desire for knowledge inside the system.

In a complex world marked by rapid, interlocking changes, knowledge becomes a crucial asset. The means to acquiring it must therefore be optimized, and people should be granted the time they need to get acquainted with and to master new technology. The paradox in our society is that in one way or another, everybody suffers from the acceleration of the time factor.

EXAMPLES

■ **AN ENGINEER WHO FAILS TO UPDATE** his or her knowledge and expertise on a regular basis becomes obsolete in less than five years.

In the cosmetics industry, things change so often, whether in the field of new, automated production technology (e.g. automatic lipstick technique costs only one third as much as traditional methods), new ingredients (through biotechnology), new formulation processes, or new, vanguard products (like Retinol).

How do we move from information to knowledge?

Since knowledge cannot be conceived of outside of human agents, for the time being, we are stuck with the problem of how to transfer knowledge. Yet a cultural dimension should also be taken into account. It is perfectly conceivable that in this respect, other cultures are more "cost-effective" than ours. Subjected to a more limited mass of information, they may have less trouble producing a higher degree of coherence in knowledge from this smaller quantity of information.

A prerequisite to creating a learning organization is identifying the mechanisms through which knowledge is acquired, the obstacles to it, and the way to make it move through the company with greater fluidity and efficiency.

We are leaving information society and entering knowledge society.

This is why the new society we are currently entering can more aptly be termed knowledge society rather than information society. It would in fact be a gross error to consider a society based on information the wave of the future. We have to leave information society in order to enter knowledge society, because information in and of itself is too mobile, too multifaceted, too ambiguous to constitute a clear-cut asset. Real competitive advantage comes from the ability to leverage information and to add significant value to it.

In this chapter, we have attempted to demonstrate that it is not so much decision-making that is crucial (since it often has an arbitrary character) as the *process* leading up to it. The reason is that *ideas are the kind of goods that only gain in value when they are shared and only wear thin when we fail to use them or prevent them from circulating.*[1]

The Importance of Education

Expenditures on training and education thus have primary strategic significance. Human resource management policies are now key to potential achievements.

People might now be able to devote more time to dreaming, imagining, and seeking inspiration.

Human time may well become time of greater duration, devoted to studious leisure. Mechanization and automation have largely freed us

---

1. *Cf.* André-Yves Portnoff, *Science et Technologie, la Révolution de l'intelligence* (1992).

from physical labor, thus enabling our minds to focus on their own workings or on the nature of matter. We must take full advantage of this new opportunity, although we don't always grasp its true implications.

The emergence of human qualities as the driving force behind innovation and business success calls for a radical change in management methods. The key task is how to break down the traditional barriers inside firms. In all likelihood, hierarchical pyramids will get flatter as companies introduce new technology. With network management, there is less need for top-heavy structures and middle management, which tends to retain and filter information. Operations will require greater participation, and through networking and E-mail, it will be possible to foster group work on a global scale.

Overarching, corporation-wide management structures will be reduced. Realizing that they can't possibly control everything from a single center, a number of companies have already made the move to set up as many as three corporate headquarters: one in the United States, one in Europe or Latin America, and one in Asia.

The new white-collar knowledge workers, who are investing in brain-power management, are blurring the traditional distinction between managers and non-managers. Leaders are no longer defined by their formal function, but by their individual behavior, because authority now conflicts with leadership. Drawing your power from your position implies maintaining the status quo, whereas leadership usually means actively organizing change. With this situation in mind, we can now assert that leadership is the keystone of competitive intelligence.

THE NEED FOR SOUL

8

What is needed is not a change of climate,
but a change of soul.

More and more companies discover that they are living in an environment over which they have no control. They are gradually losing any hope of being able to influence events in their favor. Defending their turf is clearly not a viable solution, since other players are bound to invade it sooner or later. In the global village, protected niches are a thing of the past.

Worldwide competition is forcing today's companies to venture beyond their familiar regions and lines of business and to forge ahead on more uncertain paths. As we have already seen, they must develop into learning organizations attuned to a variety of contexts, to every aspect of their environment, if they want to achieve long-term success. This brings us to the crucial role played by leadership.

Pressure to change also provides management
with a new lever.

What companies will have to strive for is not so much frenetic improvement in their value chain as a new way to weave their web according to available opportunities, in order to create what has been referred to as the "value web." And the major challenge they now face consists of "managing change," i.e. not only steering the business through turbulent times, but also using change as a management tool for generating lasting growth and efficiency.[1]

---

1. On this subject, see Richard Pascale, *Organizational Agility*, "The 21st Century" (CEO, 1996).

As we pointed out in Chapter 1, most of today's organizations are the product of their age, of the size they have reached, of their competitive intensity, and of their long-range developmental curve. If a company fails to seize the opportunity to push this curve upwards, it will probably tend toward general decline, even though it may continue to grow in the short run. The vital indicators start to look sluggish, the widespread feeling that the firm is falling out of step with its environment generates stress, and waning satisfaction leads to disillusionment.

To recover the competitive edge, such firms must not only scan the environment in search of immaterial factors, but also come to terms with the intangibles in their own line of work and detect all the habitual reflexes that stand in the way of dynamic growth.

> *The leader is the one most capable of detecting*
> *intangibles.*

Although sometimes hard to identify, the intangible aspects of any company should be analyzed just as carefully as the tangible, more readily quantifiable aspects. Whenever one of several firms that look similar on paper does noticeably better than the others, it is a good idea to compare their leadership. If, in particular, the more successful company shows greater agility and resilience, you can be sure that the leader's exceptional drive has enabled it to "model its intangibles."

The leader is the person most capable of detecting the intangible factors at work in the organization. Compelled to develop a global vision, he or she has the responsibility for accurately defining the policies best able to harness the energy of everyone involved.

A particular kind of leadership seems best suited to distilling such drive. We can distinguish three major leadership profiles.

• **Doers.** These are people who know how to learn from the past and analyze the present. They developed this ability in the context of problem solving, a level they have nonetheless had to transcend. The quickening pace of change has taught them to be proactive.

• **Strategists.** They have learned to anticipate the near future, becoming gradually more sensitive to the need for managing ambiguity.

• **Visionaries.** As we enter the twenty-first century, we still lack the invaluable ability to foresee the direction in which the world is going, the very ability that today's companies so desperately need.

Vision, or Instilling The Will to Change

The term "reverse thinking" refers to the ability to envision the future, to imagine what the company could or should look like ten or twenty years from now. Adjusting present behavior to fit in with future expectations instead of extrapolating the future from present trends clearly requires vision.

It is this ability to envision the future that should guide the choices we make today. In the current situation of change and turmoil, we need a vision that responds to our queries and doubts, while creating a powerful current that unites and mobilizes company members behind a common banner.

The Benefits of Vision

The concept of strategic vision seems much clearer if we start out from the assumption that we have to derive the present from the future. A solid vision of the future makes it possible to set up guidelines for current action.

Challenging the whole company to provide precise answers to the question, "How do you imagine us ten years down the line?", helps to clear up a good many apparent dilemmas and to sustain a kind of positive, almost irresistible drive toward the goals selected. If the leader succeeds in depicting a future that jibes with what the rest of the organization is thinking, one that everyone can readily visualize and endorse, then that future becomes the company's guiding star and focal point.

EXAMPLE

■ **PRESIDENT KENNEDY'S VISION** of American space policy was both simple and capable of stirring the entire nation. He said, "By the end of the 1970s, an American will have to have walked on the moon."

What is a Vision?

A vision is an ideal image of a desirable future for the organisation. The project behind it can be highly ambitious, like the desire to make PCs available to all households in a country, or firmly rooted in down-to-earth operations, like cutting cycle time.

EXAMPLE

■ **THE FRENCH MAIL-ORDER HOUSE LA REDOUTE** has focused all its efforts on improving service on its 48-hour delivery program. The company has chosen to differentiate itself through the message it sends customers on rapid delivery.

A vision takes shape in a process through which the company gets "reinvented." This process involves analyzing the present, studying current and future trends in the environment, creating a shared dream, and defining a strategy for change. For the vision to work and to last, however, everyone must have a clear idea of the "access gate" chosen for getting there. Otherwise, the company runs the risk of falling into a state of fuzzy confusion.

First and foremost, a vision must be widely
shared.

A number of American firms have developed the concept of "vision." They attempt to link short-term assignments to an overarching goal, which enables company members to identify with an image of the future. In France, companies unfortunately tend to confine themselves to selling products, while failing to instil any sense of a higher purpose in their people.

For this approach to work, all team members must be convinced that change is necessary and beneficial both to the company and to themselves.

People today are torn between the demand for results placed upon them by the firms employing them and the desire for personal fulfillment, which their work lives do not adequately meet. Companies should strive to bring about convergence between their goals and the aspirations of their members. This is where vision comes in—by giving meaning to work, communicating the firm's overall strategy, and creating a positive image of a shared future.

EXAMPLES

■ **WHEN PHILIPS CAME UPON HARD TIMES,** Jim Timmer, its recently appointed CEO, realized that severe cutbacks were required, but he couldn't take the time to involve everyone in a broad campaign for thinking things through. And since middle management failed to grasp the urgent necessity of change, the cutbacks were basically carried out against the opinion of most company members. The entire workforce suffered from a serious drop in motivation that would never have been so extreme if top management had bothered to explain what was at stake and what was to be accomplished. So Jim Timmer came across in the media as a real "butcher," although the desire to save the firm was what motivated him.

■ **PROMOD, A FRENCH APPAREL MANUFACTURER,** was a victim of its own success. Following a period in which it grew by leaps and bounds, the firm found itself in trouble and had to put a stop to its extravagant diversification policy. Promod decided to get back to its core business and to define the goal of diversification in geographical terms rather than in relation to products.

The problem facing the CEO was how to communicate his new, European vision to the rest of the company. He was well aware that the major gap between the requirements of massive restructuring and the expectations of worried employees would inevitably create tension. Thus, the CEO took the initiative and launched a series of in-house "press conferences" at the various units in which he fielded questions from all company members. This approach enabled him to regain their support and to restore an internal cohesion that was threatened by rising mistrust.

> *Vision constitutes the bridge between a firm's*
> *past and future.*

Competitive intelligence provides a company with guidelines, with markers that point the way toward creating or redefining vision. Vision can be particularly helpful in times of crisis. It serves to remind us of why we have adopted specific policies, by referring to the company's history, or even going back to the roots of its trademark. In a more general sense, a firm forges its vision in light of economic, social, ecological, technological, and political developments.

Here are a few examples of companies operating on the basis of an effective, sustained vision.

EXAMPLES

■ **FOUNDED IN 1850, LEVI STRAUSS** is one of those American companies that have become veritable symbols, companies that have created products embodying a global life style and consistently positioned themselves in the vanguard. The firm embarked on a course of bold innovation by having blacks and whites work together in the same factories as early as the 1950s. Levi Strauss is now widely recognized for its active concern for important social issues such as AIDS and human rights.

■ **THE CHAIN STORE NORDSTROM** has become a benchmark company in terms of customer service. Created in 1901 by a Swedish immigrant in Seattle, Nordstrom sticks to one basic rule: showing common sense in every situation in order to give the customer "an unforgettable experience" that he or she would like to have over and over again. It is this rule that has earned the firm its reputation for exceptional service.

Cultivating Agility, or Internal Intelligence

In the past twenty years, the mainspring of competitive strength has shifted from product to process and structure. Today's flexible, profitable, practically oriented units are better equipped to adapt to their environment. An agile organization is one that is trained to respond quickly, cohesively, and thoroughly to any and all market circumstances.

In a world in constant upheaval, the challenge is to be able to keep moving and learning from experience, while remaining yourself. The concept of agility was developed by the noted professor Richard Pascale [1] as a means to define and measure our ability to evolve, which is a crucial source of competitive advantage, and to translate this requirement in terms of structure.

Agility—the ability to modify your behavior faster than your rival —has become the key to success. Organizational agility allows a company to identify and take advantage of opportunities faster, and thereby to overcome its own difficulties. Finding the business exciting, keeping a lookout for new opportunities, focusing on rapid reaction, eagerly experimenting with new possibilities are the hallmarks of the agile company.

The Agility Check-up

Agile companies tend to be recent creations or start-ups. In the early phases, everyone identifies with the firm, welding it into a homogeneous unit. The concept of agility leads us to wonder whether this frame of mind can be cultivated in larger companies. Success and development often affect a firm's cultural cohesion and reduce its agility. With growth comes a gradual, imperceptible shift in the original components of the corporate culture.

The degree of agility displayed by a company can be assessed in the same fashion as with an individual. During a check-up, a doctor tests the quality of the patient's reflexes, and the same thing goes for a company. Competitive strength is conditioned first and foremost by the

---

1. The notion of agility presented here draws on a book by Richard Pascale, *Changing the Way We Change*, as well as several MCE (Management Center of Europa) seminars held in London and Brussels in 1996 and 1997.

nature of power in the firm (its limits, and the notion of authority that prevails), then by the notion of identity and the way in which people react to difficulties and conflicts, and lastly by the extent to which the firm is open to change.

On an intangible, psychological plane, the "patient's case history" will involve the following four points.

- Are employees creative, driven by enthusiasm in a kind of success mania?
- How do employees define themselves, and with what do they identify–their careers or their company?
- How does the company deal with differences and difficulties?
- How does the company take to new ideas?

Creative discomfort pushes you to strive for
ever better results.

The trick to agility is to create a chronic, yet beneficial state of discomfort that conveys the message that "There is still room for improvement."

EXAMPLES

- ■ **PHILIPS** chose the slogan "Let's make things better" in its media and billboard campaigns.
- ■ **NIKE** uses the metaphor of world-class athletes to stimulate its people to achieve higher performance levels, along with the slogan "Just do it." It would be hard to imagine a more apt way of illustrating the dynamics of success than through a reference to sports. As soon as a record is set, the challengers devote all their efforts to breaking it.

An organization's agility lies in its culture.

Today's companies derive their strength much more from their culture and their sense of purpose than from one-shot achievements. In the course of their working lives, employees have to develop qualities that can be subsumed under the heading "being," in addition to the practical skills ("doing") required by their particular field.

The strength represented by a corporate culture and a company's fundamental sense of purpose are two immaterial elements that we can't influence unless we grasp the correlation between them and other cultural elements like power relations, a sense of conflict and how to resolve it, and the way in which company members perceive their collective identity.

EXAMPLE

■ THE SUCCESS OF FAMILY MODELS can be observed today in the performance of family businesses. "In these companies, fringe benefit payments to employees and efforts at ongoing training are greater than in average firms. With better internal management, family businesses also achieve remarkable stock market results." [1]

Far from subordinating the individual to the group, agility contributes to personal development.

Large corporations that possess several strategic business units often choose to measure performance in a generic, undifferentiated fashion, even though the results may fly in the face of the actual conditions prevailing in the various businesses. This vain desire for standardization, which disregards what is really happening in the field, is diametrically opposed to the idea of agility. An agile firm makes sure that every employee understands the relation between his or her specific activity and larger, company-wide objectives.

Companies used to function in keeping with a mechanistic view of the world, in which all attempts at streamlining structures or improving labor relations were motivated solely by a desire for greater efficiency. Today, however, the human factor must serve as a touchstone for thinking about organization and performance.

Among the specific qualities associated with leadership, one that particularly stands out is an awareness of interdependence. Contrary to what is widely believed, "soft" skills like having confidence in the ability of others, acknowledging their contribution, and showing thoughtful concern for members of the team seem to be more decisive in the long run than the more common, "hard" qualities like knowing how to boost sales or to convey a sense of urgency in crisis situations. However necessary these traditional business skills may be, they are not enough, in and of themselves, to constitute what is called charisma.

---

1. *Les Echos*, February 24, 1997.

THE ENTREPRENEUR'S YOGA, ACCORDING TO RICHARD PASCALE

Richard Pascale has listed seven disciplines needed to stay agile, and thus creative, seven attitudes that will be key to success in the future.

- **Refusing the comfort of the status quo:**
- Internalizing the idea that "We can always do better."
- Knowing that your lead will soon be caught up with (just as an athlete's latest record becomes the new minimum level that everyone must attain to).
- **Managing the present in terms of the future:**
- Making assumptions about the future on the basis of past experience and current forecasts. The future thus becomes a rallying point for motivating everyone.
- Stimulating the interest of employees in creating a future together, a project to which they can contribute each and every day.
- **Showing greater fairness in discussion:**
- Fostering mutual trust and respect in the exchange of ideas.
- Questioning "the unquestionable," raising taboo subjects.
- Empowering younger company members to talk openly and freely with their superiors.
- **Developing a broad vision of the company:**
- Moving people around between the various functions to help them gain a broader vision of the firm (e.g. R & D engineers could spend several months in the company of salespeople in order to get a clearer idea of their needs).
- **Encouraging responsibility in action:**
- Accepting improvisation.
- Getting employees involved.
- Avoiding the tendency to blame "the other team."
- **Fostering relations of give and take between people:**
- Giving employees free access to information (over and above annual reports).
- Taking their career aspirations into account so that they can all derive fulfillment from their jobs.
- **Calling yourself into question:**
- Considering self-questioning a model for thinking things through, an opportunity to become aware of the need for change.
- Showing good judgment.

At this stage, we need to answer the following questions.

• Where do we want to concentrate the most energy in an agile organization?

• How do we win support for this broad goal from all company members?

The Leader and Agility

You can't renew a company without modifying the behavior of the people that make it up. Management often starts ad hoc programs in order to liven up the atmosphere, but the trouble is that people are basically conservative (although they may not know it), and they don't really like to change. The climate created by the leader is therefore essential. It can generate either a desire to take initiatives or a passive clinging to present conditions.

The leader who knows how to formulate a shared vision creates a pleasant, stimulating atmosphere imbued with optimism, one in which constraining controls and procedures are no longer of any use. The resulting enthusiasm translates into voluntary commitment.

Agility proves to be a vital skill that can change not only the way we do things, but also the way we are. It helps to reestablish social ties within the company. But staying agile requires dogged persistence and unflagging commitment on the part of leaders.

Using adversity to bounce back.

Let's take a look at the essential role played by agile leaders in dealing with adversity. They need the following qualities.

• Good judgment, i.e. the ability to perceive the way in which adversity spawns regression.

• Opportunism in resurfacing, i.e. the ability to take advantage of difficulties to strengthen the company.

• Resilience.

Meeting these three requirements, creating a vision, communicating it, and keeping it alive all depend on leadership and the way it works. Failure is often due to a lack of coherence at top management level.

Toward a new management.

In an article in its November 1996 issue on how America has renewed its companies, the French magazine *L'Expansion* listed four golden rules.

1. Combining vision with investment.
2. Inventing offers that create demand.
3. Constantly changing in order to last.
4. Getting people to dream.

According to the article, if one of these factors is missing, even decisions based on the most efficiently processed and widely circulated information will not produce the desired results. Either the process of change will soon come to nothing, or management will force employees to change without consulting them, thereby creating considerable anxiety. In either case, the firm will be off to a bad start.

In Europe, we often run into trouble because line managers tend to demand tangible proof and refuse to submit meekly to directives from above.

The "Rambo" style, with its macho cost-cutting, downsizing syndrome, must be replaced by the "judo" style. The main difference between the two will probably be less apparent at the top of the pyramid than at the upper-intermediate levels. In the future, companies will more actively seek out facilitators and coaches who know how to listen and to set up processes that get others involved.

The Leader as Linchpin of Competitive Intelligence

Even before the industrial era, traditional, command-and-control management styles were already being weakened by the development of urban civilization, which led to growing individualization. Now, in the knowledge economy, such methods are completely breaking down.

This shift is sometimes interpreted as a loss of clear reference points. The boss, that once emblematic figure, is no longer fulfilling his regulatory function, people in charge are often challenged, and everyone senses a lack of leadership. In addition, the current atmosphere of economic crisis has lowered the credibility of elites, because those that continue to apply outdated recipes for success appear doomed to fail. It becomes nearly impossible to have confidence in decision-makers who seem incapable of understanding the roots of the crisis, much less providing viable solutions.

Elites that were schooled in the values of an earlier period but that fail to engage in a large-scale effort at bringing themselves up to date can't grasp a future to which they don't hold the keys. Above all, they can't personify it, because they have a hard time encouraging people to move forward together, articulating a vision that others can share, and achieving consensus on the basis of an open dialogue with everyone concerned.

> *The icon of the star has replaced the symbolism*
> *of the boss.*

In a world in which icons are very much in the limelight, owing to new information technology, the media present show-biz stars and top-level athletes as role models. The way in which they are currently idolized serves to distract people from the deep, underlying crisis in our civilization, without, however, being able to do anything to alleviate it.

We lack an alternative project that could enable us to break with today's grim mood of despair, because we lack leaders who argue convincingly for the need to change and to take risks, leaders who can create consensus around a long-term scenario that is acceptable to all the different stakeholders. To foster innovation, you can't just confine yourself to setting up appropriate management, employment, and compensation schemes. You also have to know how to communicate in order to gain active support for common goals, while giving meaning to the contribution of every single employee.

EXAMPLE

■ **MOBILIZING THE WHOLE COMPANY BEHIND THE IDEA OF PRODUCT OR SERVICE QUALITY** as the ultimate goal, over and above profit, is the cornerstone of TQM (total quality management). The question, however, is to what extent TQM can fit in with the aspirations of employees, whose support is essential to making it work. Employees may very well consider the "quality mystique" a form of exploitation that is no less oppressive than the frenetic drive for profit. Thus, expecting them to give their bodies and souls to maximize quality seems just as unrealistic as expecting them to do so to maximize shareholder value. They are more likely to mobilize behind a major project, a good cause that goes beyond mere quality, that fires their imagination and elicits their wholehearted commitment.

Authority now conflicts with leadership.

Today, we need a different kind of leadership from the kind that prevailed during the postwar boom period. The winning organization now looks more like a jazz orchestra or a soccer team than like the conventional patterns to be found in most companies.

Leadership depends on a set of skills that are not usually associated with the world of profit-making. Although a number of traditional capabilities such as planning and setting goals are still required, in the last analysis, they are not what separates the true leaders from the others.

■ **THE CHARISMA AND INVENTIVENESS EVINCED BY THE DIRECTOR OF SOUTHWEST AIRLINES** have enabled the company to chalk up astonishing results on the civil aviation market. Owing to his impetus, Southwest employees have developed a unique blend of drive and excitement that ensures the strength of the corporate culture.

There are any number of agile, imposing leaders in corporations around the world. They include Richard Branson, Percy Barnavik, Bill Gates, Ratan Tata, Andy Grove, Jack Welch, Claude Bébéar, Lindsay Owen-Jones, and Jean-Marie Messier.

■ **HEWLETT-PACKARD'S CEO LEWIS PLATT** sees himself as someone who unearths new opportunities located at the junction between the firm's different businesses. Present in areas like computers, communications, and medical equipment, Hewlett-Packard never fails to take advantage of potential synergy between its lines of work.

The company boasts a universally recognized innovation culture and seeks to develop all the internal as well as external resources that support it. In addition to the all too often neglected opportunities at the boundaries between lines of business, HP looks for interfaces and blank spaces that can be exploited on a partnership basis, rather than trying to exert direct control over the various activities. The people at Hewlett-Packard have never aimed at imposing a unified system, much less a standard. Instead, they attempt to produce innovative components so that the firm will be actively sought out as a partner in all the businesses in which it operates.

Lastly, as far as life inside the company is concerned, Lewis Platt has unquestionably succeeded in pushing his firm's remarkable agility even further by encouraging everyone to rethink the organization in terms of the latest socioeconomic trends. Needless to say, this organizational creativity is ideally suited to an industry geared to constantly shifting technological innovation.

In the information era, which places a premium on knowledge, the kind of leader required will no longer be an energetic person capable of leading his or her troops to goals they haven't always chosen themselves. Leaders will have to be good listeners, skilled in circulating information and in encouraging interactive relations–very much like politicians who espouse noble goals that voters may not have thought of in advance but that they seem to be willing to support.

The vision projected by leaders cannot be limited in scope to a specific group. It has to concern all possible stakeholders, including consumers, employees, investors, the local community, the nation, and even all of humanity.

If we bear in mind that employees tend to treat customers the way they themselves are treated by their superiors, we should have little trouble in determining what needs to be done so that customers receive proper treatment. Leaders must make sure that all employees develop new skills, that ongoing education brings them a sense of fulfillment and a chance to realize their potential, not only as workers on the job, but also in their personal lives, as human beings.

EXAMPLE

■ LARGE CORPORATIONS like General Electric and AT&T succeeded in only a few months' time in setting up effective retraining programs for thousands of workers.

Less hierarchy means more trust.

The leader should operate more like a coach than a sergeant. This involves the following.

• Communicating lofty goals through metaphors and images that everyone is free to interpret in his or her own fashion, and rousing people to commitment.

• Developing and communicating shared values that serve to underpin commitment.

• Building and running a non-hierarchical structure in order to eliminate fear, establish trust, and develop cooperation.

• Fostering knowledge, while making sure that everyone has unlimited access to such knowledge as well as to information and communication.

The Art of Meeting Conflicting Requirements

Today's leaders must constantly operate in ambiguous, contradictory situations. This entails several obligations.

• Balancing short-term imperatives with the investment in time and resources that lasting success requires.

- Making the uncertainty of innovation compatible with the need for stability, control, and preservation of past achievements.
- Harmonizing the tangible and the intangible.
- Meeting both internal and external requirements, however conflicting they may be.
- Stressing the idea that quality by no means conflicts with cost-cutting, that the two go hand in hand.

Leaders must be fully aware of the need to set an example. They can't ask their people to change unless they themselves show active involvement in the change process.

> *The need to get involved and to step back at the same time is one of leadership's many paradoxes.*

A leader's job is full of paradox. Leaders must show intuition and inspiration as well as a rational, scientific bent. They have to be both tough and humane in the way they treat their people. And they need to combine enthusiastic daring with an ability to step back and wait things out.

> *Final decisions must be made by the whole team.*

Providential heroes belong to a bygone era. There is growing awareness today for the need to find collective solutions. Although leaders must act resolutely and vigorously, they can't come across as arbitrary or opposed to the autonomy of others. All participants should have the sense that they contributed in some way to the leader's decision.

> *The only talent essential to leaders is the ability to develop talent–in others.*

The leader of a large corporation is not a creator in the way that other people are. His or her job does not consist of producing, but of choosing and recognizing excellence. Although truly outstanding work is achieved by unique individuals operating on an equal footing, there must always be someone who takes charge of organizing and coordinating the brilliant contributions of others. Creative collaboration thus requires a maestro to conduct the ensemble.

The leader's thorough understanding of the task at hand should induce him or her to create the environment most conducive to carrying it out. In this way, the leader will win the confidence of everyone involved. (Walt Disney was an irritable, somber man, but the people who worked for him knew that his creative choices were almost always perfect.) As strong believers in dialogue, leaders have to stimulate the talents of all team members in order to empower them to work in the spirit of the firm.

To paraphrase Lao-tse, "A bad leader is a leader that everyone scorns. A good leader is a leader that everyone praises. A great leader is a leader that gives everyone the satisfaction of being able to say, "We've done it!""

Improvising, Taking Risks, Accepting Failure

According to conventional wisdom, all you had to do was "stick to the knitting" and make sure your knitting was good. Today, however, we have to learn how to forge ahead into uncharted territories, to shake off our comfortable, conformist ways, and to "ad lib" in unfamiliar countries or with confusing technologies. Leaders can no longer afford to stay on the beaten path.

The ability to improvise may well become one of the keys to management success in the complex, chaotic world we live in. At the Davos Forum in 1996, a jazz musician explained the phenomenon of personal improvisation. This led to a discussion on several subjects like shifting from the known to the unknown and being able to stray from the safety of familiar areas.

How do you know whether your improvisations are any good? "When it's got a good groove, harmonically and rhythmically, one thing leads naturally to another. That's when you can feel that it's working," answered the jazz musician.

Internet offers a field for constant
improvisation.

Internet is a model of free expression, owing to its informal character, to the absence of any hierarchy or regulation, and to the widespread conviction that it is vital for everyone to be able to participate in the free circulation of ideas.

The question, however, is why this creative flowering should be circumscribed to the Web. This kind of interface could also be introduced into our traditional structures. Creativity can emerge from the most ordinary questions like "Why?" or "Why not?" Pursuing questions to their ultimate conclusion leads to wisdom. We can learn more by examining the questions than by actually answering them.

There is nothing riskier than never taking any
risks.

Scanning activity, which Gaston Berger once defined as "reflecting in order to envision present action in the light of possible outcomes", signifies taking risks. It turns out to be less risky to take a chance on absolute novelty than to cling blindly to the status quo.

Risks should be taken consciously and deliberately. The important thing is to see them as positive opportunities. Unfortunately, this point of view is not very widespread.

TEST YOUR ABILITY [1]

Can you...

- ...constitute and motivate a team to realize your vision, based more on strategic choice than on tactical skill?

- ...see the way in which the rules of the game are changing and act in a global context?

- ...treat others with respect, while facing up to the necessity of making decisions?

- ...draw on a large pool of experience and on talent developed elsewhere than in prestigious schools?

- ...understand that internal company values must reflect external necessities, starting with customer service?

- ...obtain motivation by other means than raises and promotions, so that everyone may participate in bringing about a creative organization?

- ...accept honest mistakes, while standing resolutely up to opposition?

- ...operate like a well-informed, technically competent opportunist?

- ...note what really works and formalize it?

- ...keep your mind open on a 360° radius?

- ...show infinite patience in listening, explaining, and assisting?

- ...make the decisions right away that will be needed five years from now?

- ...bear constantly in mind that the past is the past?

We can learn a lot of valuable lessons from a willingness to take risks and to recognize the right to fail. Improvising requires a great deal of trust. In this respect, today's challenges are to overcome our fears and recognize that they exist essentially in our minds; to know how to rebuild confidence in the wake of failure; to encourage interaction between groups and participation at all levels of the organization; and to tap people's creative potential.

---

1. Based on Mike Johnson, *Managing in the Next Millenium* (Butterworth, Heinemann, Lt., 1995), p. 65-66.

Mutual Commitment to Developing Creative Co-responsibility

Only mutual relations make it possible to move from vision to practical reality. Leaders cannot mobilize the whole team behind general policies stemming from an overarching vision unless every member of the group feels responsible for making them work. Long-standing formulas like profit sharing serve exactly the same purpose, i.e. inducing every employee to act as though he or she were part-owner of the company. Similar solutions, but which go even further in this direction, must be invented and stipulated by contract.

A leader has to understand the explicit goals and underlying aims pursued by employees. Are they just interested in their pay-checks, or are they willing to give that extra ounce of energy and commitment that may make all the difference to companies like ABB, L'Oréal, Nordstrom, AXA, Levi Strauss, and Carrefour?

Mutual commitment is what can give a company the competitive edge. In order to produce that extra bit of effort, every employee should be able to grasp the connection between his or her performance and the company's bottom line.

The main thing is figuring out how to sidestep the dead weight of passive attachment to the present. In a stiflingly uniform framework of full-time work with fixed schedules, people feel little inclination to go beyond their job descriptions. They even tend to do less than what such official definitions allow for.

In contrast, flex-time arrangements and almost "customized" schedules offer considerable possibilities to those who want to increase their commitment. In such cases, we can expect to see the emergence of a sense of reciprocity that will reveal its full significance the day the company gets into trouble. This sort of positive, mutual feeling between a company and its employees must also characterize relations between employees themselves, so that people with highly different positions can nonetheless engage in harmonious cooperation. It is impossible to overcome adversity without direct human contact. The best way to achieve this, however, is by granting each person the greatest possible leeway to determine how far his or her commitment will go.

In managing creative staff, the first virtue of a leader is patience.

However urgent short-term economic imperatives may be, we have to learn how to be more patient regarding the results we expect from creative people. Creativity is something that only pays off in the long run. And although we can't measure it, we can assess it.

Thus, without rushing creative people, who need the freedom and flexibility to be themselves, we can stimulate and facilitate their work by automating the most routine operations they do. When a dream finally appears to be a realistic possibility, a new dynamic movement starts. What counts at that point is feeling rather than thinking.

We must be architects of progress instead of guardians of structure.

It is vital to instil a sense of belonging into employees. Only a general climate of well-being can generate a strong creative current.

The leaders of tomorrow will have to be skilled in developing trust –what Hervé Seyriex refers to as "zero contempt." This is no minor change, since our entire system is based on distrust. It is this fundamental lack of trust that explains why companies insist on establishing elaborate rules and regulations for meticulously supervising lower-level employees, who are reduced to the status of interchangeable order-takers.

The manager working mainly with methods, procedures, and controls was at home in a world of uniformity. But in the more complex world of today, such a manager will be replaced by the highly reactive, agile leader who knows how to listen, to communicate, and to question his or her own assumptions. This kind of leader derives authority from competence and behavior rather than from position.

Sumatra Goshal once made a very apt remark that may serve to summarize this chapter. Compelled to foster creativity and to pursue new opportunities, tomorrow's leaders must change from "guardians of structure to architects of progress."

FEELING AT HOME BETWEEN CIVILIZATIONS

The obligation for today's companies to operate on a global scale means that they have to take into account a vast array of situations around the world in order to be able to collect information, process it, and integrate it. Struggling to understand different, unfamiliar contexts is the primary imperative of competitive intelligence. You can't hope to survive and benefit from potential new sources of growth (where the opportunities are commensurate with the difficulties) without engaging in systematic scanning activity, including monitoring everything your competitors in other regions of the world are up to.

In light of growing globalization, companies must practice multifaceted scanning. To stay competitive, they have to be "on good terms" with their environment. This new requirement often leads firms to rethink their structures in order to take a broader, more complex set of criteria into consideration. For this reason, the term "competitive intelligence" seems particularly appropriate.

The Global Firm in Search of Local Connections

The most promising new growth markets now tend to be located in regions whose customs, beliefs, and aspirations are quite different from those found in the West. Yet no company can achieve satisfying results in a country without incorporating local talent. And to attract such people, you need a thorough understanding of the local context, since the particular brand of capitalism prevailing there is the product of centuries of cultural history.

Traditionally, Westerners have taken for granted the universal character of their beliefs and systems. Thus, when they first encountered non-Western societies, they attempted to impose their models on peoples they considered less advanced, if not downright "backward." At present, however, interaction between a dizzying variety of civilizations that are sometimes diametrically opposed, each one with its own form of capitalism, highlights the need for peaceful coexistence. The essential point is to strike a balance between global concerns and local interests. In this connection, it should be stressed that the ideology of progress, which has profoundly marked Western civilization over the past hundred years, is beginning to be questioned.

The End of Progressivism

The resurgence of a "civilization consciousness" would appear to be closely linked to the present era's disenchantment with the ideology of progress.[1] To put it differently: far from being an inevitable product of any coexistence between civilizations, culture clash results above all from the encounter between non-Western cultures and the Western ideology of progress.

However normal and necessary the notion of a homogenizing progress may seem to us, we should bear in mind that Asia has been the theater of interaction and coexistence between different civilizations for over a thousand years. A relationship of domination-submission only emerged clearly when these civilizations met up with modern Western civilization.

Our analysis of the clash of civilizations [2] leads us to view the past forty years as a period of conflict between two extreme versions of the ideology of progress: socialism and neoclassical capitalism. Both systems aimed primarily at the rapid increase and equitable distribution of material wealth.

According to the Western neoclassical paradigm, the emergence of the consumer as protagonist in the socio-economic system had laid the groundwork for an essentially middle-class society that would enjoy great overall stability. Consumers also constituted the linchpin of political democracy, ensuring their sovereignty through participation in elections. Mass consumption and mass democracy thus gave rise to a welfare state whose purpose was to satisfy the needs of the many. Economics, dedicated to the efficient allocation of resources or optimization of material well-being, came to have pride of place in the

---

1. *Cf.* Eisuke Sakakibara, "The End of Progressivism," *Foreign Affairs*, Sept.-Oct. 1995.
2. On this subject, see Samuel Huntington, *The Clash of Civilizations and the Remaking of World Order* (Simon & Schuster, 1996).

world of the social sciences. Technological innovation and economic growth had become the key concepts in the neoclassical scheme of things.

In the last analysis, the cold war turns out to have been little more than a civil war waged within the framework of a single Western ideology–the ideology of progress. The demise of socialism and the waning of the cold war have freed the world from this confrontation, and thereby spurred humanity on to deal with the more fundamental question of peaceful coexistence between different civilizations, whose ideologies and value systems are much more heterogeneous. Human beings can only live side by side with each other as well as with nature if a concern for balance replaces the relentless pursuit of progress.

Ever since the Renaissance, Western civilization has been predicated on the idea of progress and continual advancement, whereas Asia tends to emphasize stability. This doesn't mean that Asians are opposed to progress. But they only accept technological progress insofar as they can superimpose it on their own history, whose continuity they seek to preserve.

In the course of our travels through Asia, we have often been struck by this difference in the way in which progress and continuity are regarded, as well as by how these concepts translate in terms of communication. Contrary to Western advertising, which usually vaunts the efficiency of the particular product, Japanese advertising stages scenes of invariance, over a backdrop of traditional culture. The goal is not so much to sell the product immediately as to start out by creating an atmosphere of trust for the consumer, and only afterwards to offer a product in keeping with this atmosphere, one that reinforces it.

> *The West must gain deeper understanding of*
> *the religious and philosophical foundations on*
> *which other civilizations have been erected.*

A number of civilizations have attempted to modernize without, however, becoming Western. Non-Western societies will continue to seek to acquire the wealth, the technology, the skills and weapons that are part of modern life, while trying to reconcile this modernity with their cultural traditions. For this reason, the West must gain deeper understanding of the religious and philosophical foundations on which other civilizations have been erected, and of the way in which people living in them conceive of their interests.

Western firms that aim to conquer these emerging markets should pay increasing attention to cultural differences. This is not to suggest that they change their basic strategic orientation, but merely that they adapt it to local conditions. In particular, Western branch managers in such countries will have to find ways to express their own cultural background that fit in with the local culture.

Identity Grounded in Civilization

Identity grounded in civilization will take on growing importance in the years to come. A civilization represents the most advanced form of cultural aggregation and the broadest basis for identity. It can be defined by both the existence of common objective elements–language, history, religion, customs, and institutions–and the subjective manner in which individuals identify themselves.

There is solid evidence for assuming that in the future, the contours of the world will depend to a large extent on the interaction between seven or eight civilizations: Western, Confucian, Japanese, Islamic, Hindu, Slavic-Orthodox, Latin American, and possibly African civilization.

There are several reasons why the most significant conflicts may well be centered on the "geological fault line" that separates civilizations.[1]

• Differences between civilizations are fundamental, because they concern history, language, traditions, religion, feelings, core values, and beliefs.

• The world is becoming a smaller place, and as a result, the trend toward interaction between civilizations is becoming more pronounced all the time.

• The processes of economic modernization and social transformation that have extended to the entire planet create increasing distance between individuals and long-standing local identities, with regard to which they paradoxically express growing nostalgia.

• The West, although still at the height of its power, is now confronted with other societies that show a growing desire–and ability–to shape the world in non-Western ways. In such countries, local elites are moving away from Western values at the same time as fashion, customs, and culture from the West (especially from America) enjoy rising popularity among the masses.

• Since cultural traits are relatively immutable, the resulting differences lend themselves much less to compromise than politically or economically rooted conflicts do. In class or ideological conflict, the key question is "Which side are you on?" In civilization conflict, the question becomes "Where are you from?" Although it is possible to be an ideological turncoat, you can't help taking your civilization everywhere you go, like the chunks of earth that stick to the soles of your shoes.

• Economic regionalism is becoming more and more pronounced. On the one hand, it reinforces "civilization consciousness" in case of

---

1. *Ibid.*

success; on the other hand, it can only triumph if it has roots in a broader, common civilization.

The people and governments of non-Western societies have ceased to be the passive victims of history, as when they were targets of Western colonialism, and have assumed their place side by side with their Western counterparts as world protagonists. The figures speak for themselves: the West has 800 million inhabitants, whereas the rest of the world is home to close to 4.7 billion people. In light of this growing weight of non-Western civilizations, the West's attempts to give universal status to its values like democracy and the free market, to maintain its military hegemony, and to assert its economic interests everywhere may well provoke stiff resistance from other civilizations.

The clash of civilizations occurs on two levels.

• At the micro-level, groups living along the fault line between civilizations enter into often violent confrontation, with the aim of gaining control over disputed territory and the other groups living on it.

• At the macro-level, nation-states born of different civilizations use every available opportunity to vie with each other, whether for military and economic power, for control over international institutions and third countries, or for the triumph of their political and religious values.

In short, civilization consciousness is making headway. Conflicts between civilizations tend to supplant other forms of conflict, particularly ideological conflict, and to constitute the main source of division in the world today. Western influence over international relations is bound to decline. It is therefore in the West's interest to strengthen the ties of cooperation and unity within its own civilization, to integrate Eastern Europe and Latin America into it, to promote and preserve cooperative relations with Russia and Japan, and to prevent purely local conflicts between civilizations from escalating into large-scale warfare (consider NATO intervention in Bosnia).

From Cultural Difference to Strategic Difference

What we need to grasp is that there are two dimensions to competition: overt and latent competition. The first dimension involves standard competition over products, services, technology, capital, information—in other words, a company's output. In the past, this overt form of rivalry dominated all thinking on economic activity. Today, however, globalization confronts us increasingly with competitors from other cultural backgrounds.

Latent competition depends on cultural factors
and on the specific form of capitalism that
result from them.

It is important to recognize that our culture affects our behavior and our world view. These cultural differences, which in turn give rise to distinct forms of capitalism, may work to our advantage or our disadvantage, depending on conditions. What we mean by *latent competition* is the relative advantage–or disadvantage–you can derive from your culture and the form of capitalism it generates. It is this latent competition that determines the ability of companies to vie with competitors whose structure and mentality are totally different from theirs.

These differences in culture and context can give rise to a wide range of strategic behavior. Holding or gaining a competitive advantage depends on the systematic analysis of all these factors and the assessment of your positions in relation to those of your rivals.

European Balance: Restructuring in Order to Last

On the whole, Europe is characterized by a socialistic form of capitalism, but with a wide variety of variations. For example, the German *konzerns* are the worldwide model for the most well-balanced firms, while state intervention distinguishes the French system. In strategic terms, top priority is given to continuity. Two thirds of the hundred largest European firms are more than one hundred years old (e.g. Philips, Saint-Gobain, Péchiney, Siemens, Bayer, Daimler-Benz). These organizations evince a solid ability to reinvent themselves, restructure, grow externally, and continually pursue their international expansion. Longevity is the focus of most European strategies.

Anglo-Saxon Laissez Faire: A Concern for the Short Term

A laissez-faire approach dominates the Anglo-Saxon form of capitalism. In the US, commercial firms are forbidden from having strong connections with banks and insurance companies. As a result, American companies overwhelmingly rely on the public to raise capital. The trouble is that stock and bondholders usually have extremely short-term interests. Businesses must produce sales growth and higher earnings every quarter to satisfy investors. The constant pressure of unfaithful shareholders skews Anglo-Saxon strategy toward short-term interests and an excessive segmentation of business units. Firms that require little capital investment and rely rather on intellectual investment (e.g. Microsoft, Spielberg) are better suited for such a system.

Asian Integration: Network Power

Modern Japan is characterized by the existence of several large groups that have holdings in 60% of all Japanese businesses. These groups are essentially vertical. Each component is in theory independent, but each owns part of the capital of the others. This serves a self-regulatory function. Each group is affiliated with a bank, a real estate company, an insurance company, and an international trade company, and they are present in all sectors of business. This structure has far-reaching consequences in terms of strategy. The strength of Japanese firms is not measured by the number of its stockholders, because Japanese companies obtain capital from their affiliated banks, which allows them to *remain free of short-term pressures*. In general, Asia superimposes Western economic models on the region's traditional cultures. This enables the Asian countries to prosper economically, while retaining their cultural identity.

THE EUROPEANS ARE CLOSER TO THE ASIANS THAN TO THE ANGLO-SAXONS

In their work *The Seven Cultures of Capitalism*, Charles Hampden-Turner and Alfons Trompenaars use a series of dilemmas presented to company directors from various cultural backgrounds. After statistical processing of the answers, they assert that the Asians (from Japan and Singapore) are, culturally speaking, much closer to the Europeans (in particular to the French) than they are to most Anglo-Saxons (e.g. Americans and Australians). The British, in contrast, belong to both Western families and therefore usually occupy an intermediate position between them.

The Appendix presents a summary of a number of the questions we consider most significant. For the time being, we will simply point out that in relation to the pairs **Competition vs. Collaboration** and **Individual Efficiency vs. Teamwork**, the three groups are clearly distinguished, with the Anglo-Saxons and Asians at opposite poles and the Europeans somewhere in between. As regards **the definition of the company as a place where profit is generated, or as a place for human relations**, the first idea brings us back to the same divisions as before, whereas two new groups emerge from the second one. The Anglo-Saxons and Northern Europeans (except for the Germans) are positioned on one side, and the Asians, the Southern Europeans, and the Germans on the other side. The first category sees the company more as a system of tasks and functions that procure a pay-check to those who perform them. The second category considers it a group of people working together in which hierarchical relations and relations between individuals predominate.

The dilemma **respect for the rules, regardless of human relations, or concern for friendship, regardless of the rules** shows a clear-cut division between the Anglo-Saxons and Northern Europeans on the one hand, and the Asians and Southern Europeans on the other hand, with the Americans and the French embodying the two extremes.

Lastly, as concerns the issue of **Consensus vs. Majority**, the Japanese and the Germans, as one might have expected, come out in favor of the first principle. The Americans and the Italians defend the second one, while the French, British, and Australians once again occupy the middle ground.

Predictably enough, the only question on which all Westerners are unanimously lined up on one side and all Asians on the other side has to do with the duration of a person's connection to a company. The idea of lifelong employment in the same firm has apparently lost none of its charm for the Asians. But here again, the Italians and the French prove to be more "Oriental" than the other Westerners.

N.B.: We have selected and reorganized in our own way the findings presented in the book by Hampden-Turner and Trompenaars. Anyone interested in the complete findings would do well to consult the original.

From Geopolitical Analysis to Corporate Structure

In the current context, marked by the clash of civilizations, the fragmentation of societies, and the increasing inability of governments to solve, or even to handle properly the social problems that have developed, many companies will have to rethink their mission and their structure.

Reevaluating Local Possibilities

Local structures show spontaneous ingenuity in dealing with breakdowns that larger systems are usually powerless to repair. On the basis of this observation, we can find a whole host of useful ideas for companies.

EXAMPLE

- **EDF-GDF,** France's state-owned gas and electricity company, found itself confronted with the following challenge: maintaining the values associated with providing a public service in the common interest, while getting ready to face serious competition and simultaneously improving service, efficiency, and productivity.

Ten years ago, EDF worked out scenarios for the future, from which it drew the following conclusions.

• Labor relations inside the company were deteriorating as a result of the juxtaposition of three general interests–France, local communities, and Europe.

• The company was experiencing difficulties because of the gap between the central offices and local realities.

Today, the company is working closely with the CIME, an organization that scouts around for all sorts of local initiatives with the intention of supporting them. Yet such initiatives do not spread simply because they have been entered into a data base. In every case, the initiative's specific features need to be analyzed on their own merits. Thus, EDF now seeks to fit in with the development of local initiatives, based on the assumption that interesting ideas arise in daily life. Every company member can request free time in order to lend support to new activities and local services.

EDF top management believes that it can't give meaning to such efforts unless it contributes to the personal growth of its employees, treating each of them at one and the same time as a member of the company and a member of the community.

A Corporate Structure in Keeping with the Global/Local Paradox

Companies operating in a global economic context should not lose sight of their local environment. We have made extensive use of Professor Garelli's writings on the dilemma of competitiveness for insights on the future of business in the light of the global/local paradox.[1]

Every country functions with two kinds of economies that are diametrically opposed.

1. An economy in which the value chain of companies must be global in scope.

2. An economy providing the goods and services bought by local consumers.

The boundary between these two types of economy is becoming increasingly blurred, and there appears to be no appropriate theory for distinguishing between what is global and what is local.

---

1. Professor Garelli, "From Competitive Enterprise to Competitive Society," *Competitiveness Report*, 1996.

This leads to a number of questions. Is the global/local distinction still key to building a competitive strategy? What are the new rules governing the two kinds of economy? What are the legitimate transfers between them? Can a new balance be achieved?

The Local Economy

The local economy has to do with everything connected to the local environment, including bakeries, butcher shops, farms, post offices, as well as any service that possesses a non-exportable social value, such as hospitals, pharmacies, and dentists' offices.

Although by far the most important of the two in the past (90% of GDP), the local economy now accounts for 60% of GDP in Europe. It will no longer be protected and will be much more exposed than in the past, but it will continue to play a vital role. Since the local economy comprises the fields of health care and environment, it has a well-defined identity to which people remain attached. In contrast, multinational corporations appear to project a more hazy image.

In local economic activities, there is little mobility. Local crafts and shops, health care, assistance to the elderly are areas untouched by foreign investors. Part of the explanation lies with the laws and regulations on these activities, which can be extremely stringent and nearly impossible for foreign corporations to decode.

> *The global and the local are not as far apart as they used to be.*

Many global companies have by now understood the need to develop competitive strategies that reflect the comparative advantages of particular countries (e.g. infrastructure, tax system, social security laws). They are showing greater interest in local economies, many of whose bastions are beginning to give way.

EXAMPLE

- **PREVIOUSLY STATE-OWNED AIRLINES AND TELECOMMUNICATIONS COMPANIES** have already been privatized in a number of countries, while in others, the process is now well under way.

We can thus observe a certain confusion between two kinds of economic architecture.

- On the one hand, large corporations now have access to previously protected national networks.

On the other hand, many smaller companies are finally gaining access to the global economy through agreements on open markets and the development of new information technology, with its profound impact on international logistics, particularly in the field of shipping.

The interesting question is what structural changes this dual phenomenon is bringing about inside businesses. For the local firms that are suddenly exposed to global influence, the incessant pursuit of performance has become a precondition for survival. If they are large enough for it to be practicable, these companies have to set up the necessary competitive intelligence scanning units, so they can manage their specific value chain on a world scale and adjust to relentless competition (including price wars).

The Rising Global Tide

Structural changes must give top priority to flexibility, with flexible production equipment that can be shifted around at low cost and used in the way that offers the greatest possible competitive advantage at any given time. Thus, whole businesses have moved from Japan to Korea, to Singapore, then on to Indonesia and India.

In the global economy, maintaining control over the value chain has ceased to be a must. What companies should be doing, however, is making careful comparisons between the cost of making alliances or subcontracting, and the cost of handling local problems themselves. One expression of this situation is the tendency toward privatization of numerous activities that were traditionally part of public service.

EXAMPLE

▪ **HOSPITALS AND SCHOOLS** now outsource subsidiary activities like cafeteria, laundry, and transportation services. The French railroad company SNCF has begun shutting down a number of less profitable lines and contracting the local transportation services to private bus companies.

Given the pressure for truly global firms to be efficient and profitable at all costs, however, many of them have started cutting back their headquarters staff and running geographically dispersed networks on a decentralized basis. As a result, most of the corporation's business winds up having little to do with the "mother country." It has become hard to tell who exactly controls the global economy, or whether multinationals still have a nationality at all.

- **ABB (ASEA BROWN BOVERI)** has a highly fragmented structure made up of several thousand units that enjoy such autonomy that they end up being viewed more or less as local firms. Corporate headquarters in Zurich employs a staff of only 150, whereas the company's annual sales are close to $50 billion.

The trouble is that, although the newly exposed sectors of the economy must struggle to stay competitive on the world market, the local economy of each country tends to be chronically in the red. The question is what price the citizens are willing to pay, how much heavier taxation they can stand, in order to benefit from what the local economy can contribute, since it provides jobs and thereby fulfills an obvious social function.

Does a local economy have to become more profitable and submit to the pressure of international competition? And if so, to what extent? Government intervention might serve to prevent drastic relocations abroad decided on merely for reasons of efficiency.

Whole sectors of the local economy have already been catapulted into the world of global relations, from health care to neighborhood mini-markets. In the first case, it is the national hospital system that takes over. In the second case, the smaller stores are bought up by huge, omnipresent chains like Walmart and Carrefour.

It is by no means clear whether the encounter between local economic rules and the imperatives of globalization is harmful or in some cases beneficial.

- **GREAT BRITAIN HAS PRIVATIZED ITS FAMILY ALLOWANCE SYSTEM.** The question is whether this represents a dysfunctional turn in global/local dynamics or, on the contrary, a wise shift from the public to the private sphere.

The rules laid down by the World Trade Organization force local markets open, something which is beneficial to a number of industries like civil aviation and telecommunications. Yet other industries such as electric power and railroads should remain an integral part of the local economy.

Sometimes, local companies operate parallel to global firms. They can now obtain supplies on the world market, using Internet and information technology to accelerate the process. Purchases abroad thus make it possible to offer more attractive prices to consumers at home. It even seems reasonable to assume that in the near future, we will be able to buy part of our equipment on the other side of the planet, at lower cost and with no cumbersome procedures. More and more consumers are already buying a number of products (e.g. CDs, books, magazines) by way of electronic commerce.

The upshot of this trend is likely to be greater price transparency–entirely to the consumer's advantage. It is therefore difficult to come out with a definitive opinion on the effects of globalization.

The Desirable Balance Between Global and Local

Every country has to safeguard its competitive strength, while restoring a harmonious balance between the demands of the global economy, born of modern technology, and the reality of the local economy, which creates jobs and social well-being. To get a better idea of what this global/local balance entails, we need to analyse the specific situation of each company, an area in which competitive intelligence proves to be quite useful.

Companies producing tangible, technically sophisticated products are better suited to a global arrangement, because the possibility of catching up quickly on technological innovation fosters alliances, mergers, and a strong focus on developing one or two outstanding brands. In businesses linked to intangibles, to local culture, or to crafts production, what counts is the diversity of available brands and the extent to which they fit in with the local environment.

Truly competitive firms are the ones that can achieve the following.
• Strike the proper balance between local and global.
• Create wealth and thereby contribute to improving social conditions.
• Manage change by maintaining a constant frame of reference, based on a set of stable values.

Globalizing corporate structures makes it possible to pursue several approaches jointly and harmoniously, in what is now known as "global sourcing." In contrast, local focus enables a company to differentiate its products and services to adapt them to a necessary cultural framework. This means that we have to think concurrently in both global and local terms. R & D, outsourcing, production, distribution, and business processes have to be reconsidered in light of this dual focus.

Can a global corporation's reason for being be
adjusted to fit in with local culture?

Any company operating on a global scale, i.e. in a variety of socio-economic systems, encounters visions of the world and of business activity that differ greatly from one environment to another (e.g. Anglo-Saxon, Germanic, Southern European, Japanese, Chinese, Indian). Although in such a complex global context, defining corporate identity is no simple task, the fact is that you can't attract the best talent in every country unless you determine what the company's reason for being is.

It is therefore up to the world's governments to think seriously about whether the rules of the game, the existing laws and institutions, are still appropriate to the new world situation, which is infinitely more complex than the preceding one. Do these rules help to create a community capable of contributing to the well-being of groups and individuals, without giving in to short-term pressures, which tend to push us in the opposite direction?

INTELLIGENCE IN THE SERVICE OF COMPETITIVE STRENGTH

10

We would like to stress at this point that concepts like "aggressive competition" and "excellence" are going out of style. Exported around the world from the United States in the 1980s, the cult of excellence first referred to business, but was subsequently extended to the individual as well. The "excellent" person is supposed to combine the virtues of perfection and success.

Although this challenge may push a few people to go beyond their own limits, it also generates considerable stress for everyone else. Beyond reach for ordinary mortals, this model has led to widespread frustration–which is why it is increasingly being rejected.

People today yearn for a more harmonious society, a trend that, among other things, takes the form of a rise in so-called feminine values (balance, intuition, cooperation), as opposed to the more "virile" outlook of "more and more" that results from the conventional notion of what competition means. This major shift is bound to manifest itself in relations between firms as well.

Economic slump and rising complexity point the way toward greater cooperation.

The famous trademarks that have earned Japan universal admiration often started out as mere labels on a unit assembled from subcontracted parts. Following the massive destruction in World War II, the country's leading economic players joined forces to form the *keiretsus*.[1] Owing to

---

1. Japanese-style conglomerates of affiliated companies.

the scarce resources they disposed of, the Japanese were more open to a global vision and to the idea of forging alliances. This also served to diminish the risk of doing business, whereas Western companies were still bogged down in their Tayloristic model.

Furthermore, the new information technology now facilitates more flexible management. A small company can easily connect up with partners from around the world.

Strategic Alliances

Outsourcing

We still tend to be too imbued with the logic of vertical integration at a time in which information technology makes it possible to outsource a large part of a firm's activities. It may well turn out that what really makes a difference is the ability to figure out what competitors outsource and what they continue to handle themselves.

EXAMPLE

- **CHRYSLER** now produces only 30% of the parts that go into making its cars (as opposed to 70% at GM and 50% at Ford).

The evolution of new information technology seems to be leading to the concept of "the virtual corporation." Every company may soon have a web of alliances aimed at procuring better raw materials and at achieving better overall quality and greater flexibility.

EXAMPLES

- **NIKE DOESN'T** own a single factory, but farms out its production, giving precise specifications to subcontractors. Coca-Cola no longer produces soft drinks, focusing instead on sales, marketing, and service. Benetton connects up all its franchised outlets via Internet. These firms are now referred to as "cybercorps."

The virtual corporation doesn't require any particular location. It depends on the transfer of information between more or less autonomous units. The goal is simply to find the best partner for the best possible deal.

■ **CHRYSLER TREATS AUSTRIA AS IF IT WERE SOMEWHERE NEAR ILLI-NOIS.** Right down to the most minute details, the automaker's plant in Graz is dependent on a regional data center located in Illinois. This arrangement was made possible by a strategic alliance between Chrysler and MCI, which handles the firm's communications system. Chrysler's forty production and assembly plants are hooked up to two regional centers as well as to a Network Control Center.[1]

We thus seem to be heading toward a network culture, which is already well under way in the United States.

"Co-opetition"

The boundary between different lines of business is rapidly disappearing. Previously distinct computer, telephone, and television technologies tend to merge into one under the impact of today's digital networks. A similar trend can be observed in the fields of health care, cosmetics, and nutrition.

To achieve synergy, companies are increasingly compelled to form strategic alliances. Rather than relying on their own capacities, they should seek to team up with several complementary partners, each of which has a particular strength to offer. In such a context, there is no shortage of choices and options.

We are witnessing a steadily rising number of jointly financed research programs and other forms of cooperation, or even "co-opetition."[2] In telecommunications, for example, the "entrance fee" is so astronomically high that no single firm can ever hope to go it alone.

Japanese companies are accustomed to cooperating in the area of basic research, even though they may be putting out rival products. The idea is that the war will resume subsequently, i.e. in the marketplace.

We can thus expect to see a "frenzy of alliances" in the digital field, followed by shifting coalitions and new, surprising forms of cooperation.

---

1. *Cf.* Francis Pisani, "Les constructeurs américains utilisent de plus en plus les technologies de la communication," *Le Monde*, November 22, 1996.
2. A neologism formed from the words *cooperation* and *competition*.

■ THE TWO MAJOR COMPUTER RIVALS IBM AND APPLE made common cause against Microsoft, while Bill Gate's firm was attempting to establish closer ties with Intel. Then, as the Mac crisis got deeper, Steve Jobs, the man who invented the personal computer, took control of the firm once again and contacted Bill Gates in the hope of gaining some additional elbow room. By purchasing 5% of Apple to the tune of $150 million, the software king showed fairly good business sense, since this enabled him to woo the intellectual and scientific community, people for whom Macintosh represents a great deal more than just a computer. In their eyes, bailing out Apple is virtually tantamount to defending freedom of speech. It is highly symptomatic that two men in their forties wearing T-shirts, two incarnations of the California myth, launch into a form of "coopetition" that would certainly not have come as easily to older, less legendary managers. For Bill Gates, this move was more than just a publicity stunt. It represented a way to gain an invaluable ally to push his program Explorer against Netscape and thereby get one step closer to conquering Internet. And IBM, for all its "wise solutions" for surfing the web, woke up to find that its offensive had been thwarted by the surprise alliance between the two "wiz kids."

■ HARD AND SOFT also combine together in the area of television. Multimedia manufacturers are attempting–with unclear success–to get a foothold in a business that is culturally quite distant from theirs: producing programs. In theory, to be sure, the major alliances occurring in the world of high tech and communications, like the buyout of Columbia by Sony, make strategic sense. Yet because of the glaring contrast in sensibility and culture between the two partners, practical application of the alliance turned out to be disappointing. Following heavy financial losses, Sony president Akio Morita threw in the sponge.

Creation of Wealth versus Social Cohesion?

When the interests of transnational corporations begin to diverge from the interests of local workers and consumers, the danger is real that consumer society will be seriously destabilized. In combination with the ecological risks of today, this economic and social gap is a source of deep concern that leads countries and companies alike to question their own vision of progress.

As regards the various threats to the environment, a number of particularly sanguine observers pin their hopes on new technological solutions. Yet this is merely the latest reincarnation of the ideology of progress. While natural scientists are struggling to understand vast systems on the basis of infinitesimal observation, it seems unlikely that we will ever be able to evaluate precisely the impact of human activity on the environment or solve ecological problems through technological innovation alone.

Similarly, economists and politicians find it increasingly difficult to convince others–or even themselves–that problems like pollution and social inequality will go away as soon as the economy picks up.

Traditionally, the main goal of companies, at least in the Western world, has been to maximize earnings per share. At present, however, there are solid grounds for believing that previously efficient models may not work so well in the future. The recent efforts of the former communist countries to import Western capitalism highlight the limits of our system. Moreover, it seems doubtful whether we can reasonably regard profit as our only objective in a world beset with deep social problems. Perhaps the time has come to consider other criteria for success.

We are confronted with a paradox. On the one hand, a company has to stay profitable in order to avoid penalizing its employees and itself. On the other hand, the pursuit of immediate returns with no ethical or ecological restrictions may penalize the firm just as much by alienating consumers. In addition to economic performance, companies will increasingly be called on to take a stand on the most important social problems of the day. If they refuse to do so, they may come across as heartless, soulless, antisocial institutions.

In a troubled Western world where the existence of nearly 35 million unemployed gives rise to a pessimistic climate, while the rest of the world has not been able to create enough jobs to accommodate an increasingly large population, the islands of prosperity (i.e. rich countries and prosperous businesses) could become the targets of the disinherited.

> *The frantic pursuit of efficiency may wind up undermining companies.*

At present, a leader is often judged according to his or her ability to scale back wages, lower suppliers' profit margins, and impose new constraints on distributors. Everyone involved understands only too well what the rules and the objectives of the competitive game really are. As a result, we find ourselves in a climate of distrust and uncertainty.

The question that immediately arises is whether everything should be sacrificed on the altar of competitiveness. How much change can a country or company take merely in order to survive in this highly competitive world? Is there a breaking point beyond which the pursuit of efficiency threatens the very survival of countries and companies alike?

The answer lies in finding a dynamic equilibrium between wealth creation and social cohesion. And that requires a new awareness of the vital role companies should now be playing in society.

The Socially Responsible Firm

Today's nation-states are confronted with increasingly serious problems, although they have only limited resources at their disposal. It follows that they will be less able than in the past to fulfill their traditional function of guaranteeing stability. Thus, businesses may be called upon more and more to take positions on the major issues facing society. As the ability of the state to address such issues continues to decline, businesses will practically be obligated to assume a large share of responsibility in dealing with the most threatening problems.

This leads us to question the laissez faire model of Adam Smith. Does his theory of a common interest ensured by the individual pursuit of happiness best serve us today, or should we invent new rules which are better adapted to the environment currently taking shape?

Reconsidering Two Hallowed Myths

To prepare for tomorrow, we might question two myths which have the character of sacred cows in the business world.

1. Is immediate profit the only goal of business, even to the detriment of long-term prosperity?

The answer to this question is an emphatic "no." The goal of a business cannot be just to make a profit. Profit is not an end in itself; it is a means to an end. It is what enables a company to achieve its objectives, i.e. to pursue its development and to meet the dictates of its overall vision.

What, then, is the purpose of a company in this new context? Charles Handy suggests that it exists "for itself." We might call it the existential company, since what it strives for is continued existence. A company only has the right to survive as long as it is doing something useful, at a cost which people can afford, and it must generate enough funds to ensure that its goods and services achieve the greatest possible development, in the sense of improving the well-being of customers.

Business "existentialism" is not, therefore, a form of selfishness. A common vision can not only provide answers to those who search for meaning, but also help to balance the often conflicting demands facing a company.

2. Are stockholders the sole owners of the company?

We certainly consider them as such, yet the decisions they make are overwhelmingly dictated by short-term concerns, especially in the

Anglo-Saxon environment. And because their short-term interests do not always correspond to the long-term interests of the firm, it may be said that shareholders have disproportionate control over the company's orientation. In fact, they can be compared to speculators or punters who are more interested in the price of the horse than in the animal itself. Does it make sense for those who provide the funds to have such influence over what management does? Perhaps the system prevailing in Japan, where stockholders are treated as preferential bondholders, provides a more balanced approach.

Employees are not the shareholders' property.

In the past, a company was essentially a set of physical assets run by people. Today, however, it depends primarily on people, who now work with non-material assets. Human potential is what determines a firm's wealth today. To put it simply, it is impossible for organizations to own some of their most important assets–their employees.

These are by no means idle quibbles. As firms attempt to attract and retain the most talented people, human resource policies and the nature of the work environment take on renewed strategic importance.

Towards a New Concept of Business

The Vital Question of Ultimate Purpose

We have often been impressed, on visits to Japan, by the time devoted to discussions on the ultimate purpose of the organization. Often, we spend more than an hour discussing a vision meant to create enthusiasm for a company's goals. It is through this kind of attention to the larger purpose (beyond profit) that we can foster a shared environment where every employee buys into our vision and feels like a true partner in the firm.

Perhaps we should start considering a global corporation as a living community in constant expansion. The concept of business might be enlarged in order to cope with the challenges of tomorrow. Charles Handy proposes a structure composed of six kinds of stakeholders whose demands on the company often conflict: shareholders, employees, customers, suppliers, the environment, and the community, i.e. the social context in which the firm operates.

The firm owes something to each of its stakeholders. This notion of conflicting complementarity between community and property would help reduce the short-term pressures typical of the current arrangement, while allowing the business to continue to produce the profits needed to benefit its community.

Networking, or the World of Tomorrow

Recently, a team at MIT developed scenarios for future organizations. All the scenarios predicted an increase in cooperative relations between separate units, whether they are part of a single large firm with a highly flexible central structure, like ABB (see the example in Ch. 9), or small companies with no legal connection to each other. In attempting to imagine the social needs that such a trend may give rise to, we have singled out the following points.

• Much of economic activity will be conducted by networks of independent contractors or very small firms working together in temporary combinations on various projects. For example, automobiles could be designed by groups of individual designers operating as independent contractors, who come together in joint ventures to form competing coalitions for exploring alternative designs for the various car components. If this scenario comes to pass, the result would be an extremely flexible way of organizing the necessary tasks.

• If the future turns out to belong to networks of small organizations, then professional associations could take care of many of the economic, social, and personal needs that were previously met by large companies. These associations could provide informal knowledge sharing, formal training programs, social networking, and various documents establishing reputations and credentials. There might also be other organizations, networks, and communities whose purpose would be to satisfy basic human needs like the need for socializing, for realizing your potential, or for giving expression to your values.

New structures would have to fill the void left by the gradual disappearance of the traditional workplace. The seeds for them may already exist in some of today's organizations like trade unions and trade associations, neighborhood groups, fraternities, and college alumni associations. Of course, a number of large corporations would still exist, and they could carry out tasks of coordination and certify the quality of products and services (especially those sold directly to consumers). But the proportion of GWP (Gross World Product) accounted for by these firms could significantly decrease. In this new environment, where everyone would be shopping around for collaborators to form networks, trust would become the chief concern.

CONCLUSION

Self-preservation should generate a healthy feeling of concern.

Why should a company worry about its future? First of all, in order to survive, and second of all, in order to grow and evolve.

Loss of competitive strength through a lack of vigilance spells death for a company. The cost is incalculable: workers, suppliers, subcontractors, and shareholders all stand to lose.

A company is a living entity.

It is appropriate to view the company as a living entity whose primary imperative is staying alive.[1] It follows that this living organism must continually adapt to its environment and explore the contingencies, risks, and opportunities to be found in the outside world.

It is by squarely facing the future that we can determine the right course.

Companies that conceive of themselves as living entities can achieve long-term success, provided they are capable of exploring their future, clearly separating this exploratory activity from their operations, disseminating power, and above all, changing.

The challenge of change crops up once again.

"The main thing is to change," said Colette. The desire or the need to change is indeed the touchstone of what we have attempted to

---

1. *Cf.* Arie de Geus, *The Living Company* (Harvard Business Press, 1997).

demonstrate throughout this book. Proper competitive intelligence implies first and foremost this desire to change, then mastery of the art of change.

In order for a company to stay in the lead and raise its performance to the level required by the volatile world of today, four essential conditions must be met.

- Strong pressure to change.
- A clear, shared vision of the direction in which the company should be going.
- A capacity for change.
- *The initial operational steps* that bear witness to a will to carry change through.

All too often, the people in charge of competitive intelligence may succeed in raising the awareness of some people, but still remain in a state of frustration. The newly acquired outlook only partially translates into action, and the initial fervor wears thin, either because people are intent on maintaining their comfortable positions or because they are simply afraid of change.

Be that as it may, everyone must realize that a short-term perspective can't possibly solve the problems of tomorrow. Just as it is an illusion for a country to believe that it can "beat its competitors on the world market" without engaging in domestic reform, a company that aims it ensuring its growth first has to endeavor to improve the quality of its values and internal structures. This is the precondition for raising the efficiency of the work performed—and it requires the self-realization of those who perform it.

Complexity offers humanity new opportunities.

Complexity is not only a destabilizing factor; it is also a force for decentralization, an encouragement to implementing the principle of subsidiarity. Thus, complexity calls for greater responsibility and can therefore stimulate individual initiative in an agile company.

Intelligent use of complexity fosters a critical attitude toward past achievements and encourages people to surpass themselves. At the same time, however, it creates a new risk—that of decision-making at all levels of the organization. Thus, in response to rising complexity, new barriers are often set up, with the upshot being greater segmentation of the company than before. A complex environment tends to secrete increasingly dense information flows as a way to maintain the organization's cohesion.

If we want this information to be useful rather than fatal, we have to invest much more time in combining knowledge and matching skills, i.e. in managing a growing number of interfaces. The ability to listen, to engage in dialogue, to establish intelligent collaboration and to do everything that falls under the heading of "internal communication" thus become the essential tools of business success today.

In this sense, complexity can enable human beings to rediscover meaning in their work, and thereby to give happiness a serious try.

THE ABC OF COMPETITIVE INTELLIGENCE (or a brief summary for those who are already convinced of its value)

1. Understand the driving forces behind change in our competitive environment.

2. Figure out how far the company will go in accepting change; take human resistance into account.

3. Attempt to break with traditional mind-sets.

4. Carry out thorough-going scanning activity, so that decisions can be based on state-of-the-art analyses (while making sure that competitors don't get there first).

5. Introduce simple measures for assessing company performance and increasing motivation.

6. Zero in on the aspects of company life that are related to values, culture, and group dynamics.

7. Strengthen the leader's role as someone who shares a vision and pushes it all the way down to the lowest levels of the company.

8. Incorporate new information and communication technology while transcending cultural obstacles; create an *ad hoc* structure to facilitate the process. Trying everything that comes out may well be the most fruitful approach, since it encourages people to question the status quo.

9. In a nutshell, listen, scan, share, and learn together, capitalizing on the potential offered by today's information technology.

10. Congratulate yourself on having introduced the previous nine points–that means you're on the right track!

APPENDIX
Differences in Cultural Perception as Revealed by the Dilemma Method

---

Summary of the Questions

N.B. We have termed *statement A* the idea that received the most votes. Only the percentages obtained by the majority response (i.e. agreement with statement A) are indicated below and in the table.

1. Competition vs. Collaboration

– *Statement A:* Fanning the flames of competition between rival firms works to the advantage of consumers, who would be penalized by excessively amicable relations between companies.

– *Statement B:* Encouraging cooperation expands markets, increases efficiency, creates more products, and reduces costs, all of which is beneficial to consumers. Cooperation on a regional scale also helps firm to deal with globalization.

– *Results:* Statement A obtains between 68% (USA) and 19% (Singapore).

2. Individual Efficiency vs. Teamwork

First question. Before hiring a person, it is more important to consider:

– *Statement A:* His or her talents, knowledge, and past achievements.

– *Statement B:* His or her ability to fit in with a previously constituted group.

– *Results:* Statement A obtains between 92% (USA) and 39% (Singapore).

Second question. Do you prefer the kind of job in which management encourages:

– *Statement A:* Individual merit and initiative, giving people the freedom to do their work.

– *Statement B:* Group efficiency, rewarding the team rather than the individual.

– *Results:* Statement A obtains between 97% (USA) and 39% (Singapore).

3. Profit vs. Human Relations

First question. Profit constitutes:

– *Statement A:* The only real aim of the company.

– *Statement B:* A means to satisfying all stakeholders, including shareholders, employees, and customers.

– *Results:* Statement A obtains between 40% (USA) and 8% (Japan).

Second question. A company is basically:

– *Statement A:* A system of tasks and functions for the performance of which appropriately skilled people are paid (through salary or outside contracting).

– *Statement B:* A group of people working together, where social relations are essential for the whole to function properly.

– *Results:* Statement A obtains 74% (USA), 35% (France), and 29% (Japan).

4. Rules vs. Human Relations

First question. Your friend has a drink with you instead of tending to his or her job, and an accident results. You are the only witness. Is it legitimate for your friend to ask you to cover for him or her?

– *Statement A:* Absolutely not.

– *Statement B:* Partially.

– *Statement C:* Certainly.

– *Results:* Statement A obtains between 94% (USA) and 53% (France).

Second question. You know that your subordinate regularly comes late to work because of family problems. Is it legitimate for this employee to ask you to support him or her in relation to his or her colleagues?

– *Statement A:* Absolutely not.

– *Statement B:* Partially.

– *Statement C:* Certainly.

– *Results:* Statement A obtains between 95% (USA) and 43% (France).

5. Consensus vs. Majority

Question. A meeting is held to appoint someone to a post. Although a majority is in favor of one name, there still are quite a few people opposed. What should be done?

– *Statement A:* Continue the discussion in order to reach a broader consensus.

– *Statement B:* Put an end to the discussion as soon as a majority has been achieved.

– *Results:* Statement A obtains 84% (Japan), 38% (USA), and 35% (Italy).

6. Connection to the Company

Question. I expect to stay with the company:
– *Statement A:* For a limited period of time.
– *Statement B:* For the rest of my working life.
– *Results:* In the West, statement A obtains between 99% (USA) and 72% (Italy); in Asia, it obtains between 41% (Japan) and 32% (Singapore).

Question	USA %	Australia %	U.-K. %	Sweden %	Netherlands %	Germany %	Italy %	France %	Japan %	Singapore %
1.	68	62	65	39	50	41	51	45	24	19
2.1°	92	91	71	53	88	87	62	57	49	39
2.2°	97	97	90	95	92	84	69	69	49	39
3.1°	40	35	33	27	26	24	28	16	8	11
3.2°	74	59	55	56	61	41	46	35	29	39
4.1°	94	91	82	89	92	90	56	53	66	59
4.2°	95	82	84	91	82	94	47	43	56	61
5	38	53	59	41	66	69	35	62	84	–
6	99	96	94	81	89	83	72	79	41	32

Imprimé en France. JOUVE, 18, rue Saint-Denis, 75001 PARIS
N° 264572G. Dépôt légal : Avril 1999